Sonia
I hope this
makes you
smile
think
and nod
knowingly!

with love
& Laughter

Dixie Aug '93

THE NAKED PHYSICIAN:
Poems about the Lives
of Patients and Doctors

EDITED BY RON CHARACH

Quarry Press

Many of the poems in *The Naked Physician* first appeared in "The Medical Poet" column in *The Medical Post*. The editor would like to thank Richard Sutherland, Features Editor, and Derek Cassels, Editor, for their assistance and support in this project.

Several poems by Ron Charach appeared in slightly different form in *Queen's Quarterly, Books in Canada, Descant, The Fiddlehead, The Antigonish Review, The New England Journal of Medicine*, and in his book *The Big Life Painting* (Quarry Press). Several poems by Kirsten Emmott have appeared in BCMA *News* and in the chapbook *Are We There Yet?*. Several poems by Arthur Clark have appeared in his book *Kinetic Mustache* (Véhicule Press). "Crocodile" by Robbie Newton Drummond appeared in *Poets 88* (Quarry Press).

This book is dedicated by the editor to Doctors Phillip Katz and Len Leven.

The publisher thanks the Ontario Arts Council and The Canada Council for assistance in publishing this book.

CANADIAN CATALOGUING IN PUBLICATION DATA

Main entry under title:

The Naked Physician : poems about the lives of patients and doctors

ISBN 0-919627-77-3

1. Physician and patient — poetry. 2. Canadian poetry (English) — 20th century. I. Charach, Ron.

PS8283.P49N34 1990   C811'.54080356   C90-090166-7
PR9195.35.P49N34 1990

Design and imaging by ECW Type & Art, Oakville, Ontario
Printed and bound in Canada by Hignell Printing, Winnipeg, Manitoba.

Distributed in Canada by the University of Toronto Press, 5201 Dufferin Street, Downsview, Ontario M3H 5T8 and in the United States of America by Bookslinger, 502 North Prior Avenue, St. Paul, Minnesota 55104.

Published by Quarry Press Inc., P.O. Box 1061, Kingston, Ontario K7L 4Y5 and P.O. Box 348, Clayton, New York 13624.

CONTENTS

Introduction

The Medical Poet *Ron Charach* 9
Shamanic Journey *Kirsten Emmott* 12

1. *Lions, Crocodiles, and Old Red Foxes:*
   The Lives of Patients

Danse Marine *J. Lalouette* 19
The Fetus Is Stopped at the Border *Kirsten Emmott* 20
Labour and Delivery *Ron Charach* 21
Birth in Inuvik *Robbie Newton Drummond* 23
Afterbirth *Vincent Hanlon* 25
The Obstetrical Patter (When Magic Fails) *Vincent Hanlon* 27
Christmas Delivery *Vincent Hanlon* 29
My Son *Ariel Boilen* 31
A Hospital for Sick Children *Heather Weir* 32
Nursery *M.A. Bramstrup* 34
Hospitalized Child *Daniel Lowe* 36
Beginning the Thaw *Ron Charach* 37
Come up to the Crib *Ron Charach* 38
Pumpkinhead *Ron Charach* 39
Failure to Thrive *Ron Charach* 40
Intensive Care *Robbie Newton Drummond* 42
Cancer of the Blood *Robbie Newton Drummond* 43

She Was a Refractory Child *Arthur Clark* 44
Stephanie *Gerry Greenstone* 45
White Laces *Ron Charach* 47
Snake *Vincent Hanlon* 49
A Lover's Quarrel *Vincent Hanlon* 51
Rubbers and Foam *Vincent Hanlon* 52
The Slim *Robbie Newton Drummond* 54

The Spirits Funnel *Mladen Seidl* 56
Trembling Delirium *Robbie Newton Drummond* 58
Thick Honey *Robbie Newton Drummond* 60
Suicide *Robbie Newton Drummond* 61
Looking for Extra Hands *Ron Charach* 62
Equipoise (How Big, How Cut, and How Hard) *Ron Charach* 63
Junkie on the Phone *Kirsten Emmott* 64
A Memorable Story *Vincent Hanlon* 65

A Lover's Prayer (Schizophrenia) *Betty Ujanen* 67
Differences *Robert W. Shepherd* 68
Internal Bleeding *Gerry Greenstone* 70
Why Not Try an Iguana *Ron Charach* 72
The Most Serious Moment of Our Lives *Ron Charach* 73
The Walking Woman *Peter Grant* 74
In the End with Mrs R. *Carl J. Rothschild* 75
On Meeting My Analyst *Heather Weir* 76

Diverticulitis *Barry Wheeler* 78
A Bitter-Sweet Removal *Barry Wheeler* 79
Open Heart Surgery *Vincent Hanlon* 80
Fears Around Her Five Pounds *Ron Charach* 86
Tic Doloreux *Ariel Boilen* 87
Foreign Body *Vincent Hanlon* 88
A Life-Saving Enterprise *Vincent Hanlon* 90
CA Sandra *Peter Grant* 91
Crocodile *Robbie Newton Drummond* 92

Twilight Exchange *Shel Krakofsky* 93
In Coronary Care *Vincent Hanlon* 94
A Cure for Old Age *Vincent Hanlon* 95
Round and Down *Joe Wiatrowski* 97
Old Fox *Ariel Boilen* 98
House Call *Elmer Abear* 99
The Long Road to the Sea *Ron Charach* 100

2. Life in the Late Hours:
The Lives of Doctors

The First Cry H.J. Goldstein 103
Back Into It Gerry Greenstone 105
It Takes All Sorts W.C. Watson 106
Cardiac Arrest Heinz Lehmann 108
Code M.A. Bramstrup 109
Code 444 Gerd Schneider 111
House Call: 3 a.m. Kirsten Emmott 112
Night Shifts Vincent Hanlon 113
Spinal Tap Gerry Greenstone 115

Primary Iatrogenic . . . Dysnomenclasia Ian Wilkinson 116
The Naming of Cells James Gough 117
Methuzelam, Confuzalem Peter Grant 118
Invasion of the Megamice Peter Grant 119
Corpus Callosum Bob Maunder 120
Kleinsteins's Pharmacy Bob Maunder 121
At the Specialist's Kirsten Emmott 123
A Poem about the Pancreas Ron Charach 125
Dummytology Ron Charach 127
Abraded Back Ron Charach 129
The Scrub Nurse Barry Wheeler 130
When Performing This Trick Arthur Clark 131
Her Last Autopsy Arthur Clark 132
Sex Therapist Practitioner Vincent Hanlon 133
The Surgeon Paul Steinhauer 134
On Taking a History Paul Steinhauer 135
Factoring the Convention Ron Charach 136
Cutting Up One Neurosurgeon Ron Charach 137

Philanthropy Basil J. Grogono 138
An Approach to Declaring the Dead Vincent Hanlon 139
Real Numbers Vincent Hanlon 141

Death of a Cowboy *Morris Gibson* 143
After the Concert *Vivian Rakoff* 144
Space-Time's Main *J.V. O'Brien* 145
While I Lay Reading Medicine *Mary Seeman* 146
What Stays Down *Ron Charach* 147
Theorem of Alienation *J. Lalouette* 148
Dead Certainty *Roy M. Salole* 149
An Apparition *Roy M. Salole* 149
The Dead *Arthur Clark* 150
In Search of Mr Green *Ron Charach* 151

Hospital Encounter *Mary Seeman* 152
A Therapist and a Rose *Dorothy Hartsell* 154
First Visit *Maurice Schwartz* 155
Stricken by Flu *Mladen Seidl* 156
I Stepped Past Your Room Today *Gerry Greenstone* 157
Inferno *Vincent Hanlon* 159
The Stethoscope's Song *Carl Lapp* 160
The Naked Physician *Ron Charach* 161
Faulkner Faltering *Ron Charach* 162

My Vision *Daniel Lowe* 166
Nazi Doctors *Daniel Lowe* 168
A Sitting Sisyphus *Shel Krakofsky* 169
In a Bicycle Repair Shop *Shel Krakofsky* 170
Church Street Bookstore *Shel Krakofsky* 171
Countertransference Call *Elmer Abear* 172
From the Clinic Window, Pond Inlet NWT *Bob Maunder* 174
Heart Song *Bob Maunder* 175
Hymn *Arthur Clark* 176
Origami *Arthur Clark* 177
Life in the Late Hours *Ron Charach* 178

Notes on Contributors

"As a writer I have never felt that medicine interfered with me but rather that it was my very food and drink, the very thing which made it possible for me to write. Was I not interested in man? There the thing was, right in front of me. I could touch it, smell it. It was myself, naked, just as it was, without a lie, telling itself to me in its own terms" (Dr William Carlos Williams, "Projective Verse and the Practice").

Several years ago I offered my services to *The Medical Post* as a kind of poet-in-residence and soon became the host of a bi-weekly column on poetry called "The Medical Poet." As a physician and a poet, I was keen to bring to light the work of other physician-poets in Canada, in part so that I would feel less lonely in my dual calling, in large so that I could show the creative character of fellow author-doctors. The column carried an open invitation to physicians to submit poems on medical themes for publication. And despite fears of receiving only medical-school limericks, the quality of the responses has been so remarkable as to warrant collecting these poems in an anthology.

The tradition of the physician-poet in our culture is venerable. The Berg Collection of "Doctors as Men of Letters" at the New York Public Library includes work by such well-known physician-poets as Thomas Linacre, Thomas Lodge, Abraham Cowley, Tobias Smollett, George Crabbe, Robert Bridges, and William Carlos Williams. Other great poets, playwrights, and novelists have sought out careers in medicine for a time, including Oliver Goldsmith, Percy Bysshe Shelley, John Keats, James Joyce, Gertrude Stein, and Robinson Jeffers. Still others have made medicine the subject of their poetry. Sylvia Plath's "Two Views of a Cadaver Room" and "Tulips" come to mind, as does British poet James Kirkup's "A Correct Compassion" and Canadian poet Alden Nowlan's "Five Days in the Hospital" (which Vincent Hanlon alludes to in this anthology in his poem "Open Heart Surgery"). Few readers will ever forget the power of Walt Whitman's "hospital" poems in *Drum-Taps*, written while he served as a volunteer medical aid during the Civil War. And some physician-poets have used their writing therapeutically, as J.B.S. Haldane does in his poem "Cancer's a Funny Thing," published in the *Oxford Anthology of English Verse* and written, according to this author-doctor, "to encourage cancer victims to get operated on sooner, and with good cheer."

As the opening epigraph from Dr William Carlos Williams suggests, physician-poets have a rare point of view that greatly enriches their work as authors. Every day in their work as doctors they see us naked. They witness our birth, they witness our death. They diagnose our illnesses, they prescribe our cures. They respond to the rhythm of our breathing with an ear as acute as that of a musician. At their best they respond to our words with an understanding as profound as that of a minister. This rare perspective not only makes the content of their poetry unique but also gives form to their verse. As William Carlos Williams brilliantly demonstrated in his own "projective verse," human breathing patterns *inform* poetic metre, determine the duration of the poetic line. The poems by physician-poets collected in the first section of this anthology on the lives of patients are so informed by this "naked" perspective.

The poems collected in the second section on the lives of doctors present the physicians in *their* naked form. We are offered a special perspective on *their* lives. Modern physicians struggle to retain their intuition, to show their empathy – even their humanity – amid the storm of machine-generated data that is modern medicine. That they often do not succeed in doing so may explain why, at a time when doctors can do more for patients than ever before, they are frequently maligned in the media and sued by their patients. Doctors learn to use a variety of methods for keeping their calm amid all the pain and suffering they face on the job. Some of these methods are adaptive, like the use of humor (light and black) or "information therapy" (immersing oneself in the facts). Some doctors use defenses that are decidedly less adaptive, as the high incidence of alcoholism, drug abuse, depression, divorce, and suicide among physicians attests. And others simply fall back on their raw humanity and expose themselves to the great risks of caring openly for their patients. The physician-poets in this collection reveal themselves to us in such various light, appearing as naked – as vulnerable, as fearful, as noble – and as human as any patient.

The Naked Physician is thus a very specialized anthology of poetry, focused on the work of a particular profession, and a very special anthology, offering us a new vision of ourselves. As a specialized book informed by the experience of working doctors, this anthology takes a place alongside the growing body of *work* poetry in Canada, such as *Going for Coffee* and other poetry collections inspired by the political and editorial activities of Tom Wayman and the Vancouver Industrial Writers' Union (Kirsten Emmott from this collection is a founding member); and complements *Sutured Words,* an anthology of poems about medicine by modern American poets. As a collection of poetry enabling us to see ourselves anew, *The Naked Physician* takes a place beside all good literature in making us more humane, more understanding of one another.

¶ *Ron Charach*

11

"Transpersonal crises of this type bear a deep resemblance to what the anthropologists have described as the *shamanic* or *initiatory* illness (Eliade, 1964). It is a dramatic episode of a nonordinary state of consciousness that marks the beginning of the career of many shamans" (Christina and Stanislav Grof, "Spiritual Emergency: the Understanding and Treatment of Transpersonal Crises").

The core experience of the shamanic journey is a profound encounter with death and subsequent rebirth.

Yes, I have encountered these. On the very first day of medical school we were escorted to the hospital, met on the wide stairs by an elder, taken to the halls of birth and death, saw a baby born, and then the morgue.

Initiatory dreams and visions include a descent into the underworld

During that first year we went every day behind the door marked "Authorized Personnel Only." Gross Lab was a private morgue for the sixty of us. Most of us had never seen death before. We were to follow it down every twist and turn it took, shred it into so many small pieces that we would lose our fears of it.

under the guidance of ancestral spirits,

Our teachers knew where the nerves and arteries lay buried. They warned us to have respect for the corpses, to study hard, and not to leave skulls on the bus.

attacks by demons,

No, not the easily enraged surgeons, nor the violent drunks in Emergency, nor the germs they carried, but our terrors, which we had to keep buried.

exposure to unimaginable emotional and physical tortures,

There was no sleep. Few meals. Internship was a year but residency was years more. Blood splashed on your shoes. People began to scream when you told them their dear one had just died.

and finally complete annihilation.

There comes a time when you know if you get one more call tonight, you will scream and pound the bedside table where the relentless phone sits and then go, stumbling with weariness, completely blank except for the little bit that remembers how to do a cardiogram or a forceps delivery.

This is then typically followed by sequences of rebirth

The babies never failed to bring it back. For those few minutes between the sight of the head, and the paperwork after, I was alive.

and ascent to supernal realms.

You can see the interns occasionally, standing at a window staring out over the city just before dawn, no longer able to think, but still able to feel, wondering what comes next.

Although there exist considerable variations in the details of these ordeals among different tribes

When I was a resident it was no better, although the rewards came more thickly; many more babies, much more abuse.

and individual shamans

There were a dozen of us and many did not notice anything odd about the way we were living, for in spirit they were still in the Gross Lab where the wishes of the "subjects" no longer existed.

they all share the general atmosphere

There was a single on call room, but there was a screen, which I could go behind to express the milk that I could no longer give my baby; the other residents would turn on their heels and walk out when they saw me.

of horror and inhuman suffering.

We were as kind as we knew how. This was not enough. There was death now and then, and considerable pain for the patients. We tried to care about them. Nobody cared about us, not even ourselves.

The tortures involve experiences of dismemberment,

Dismemberment. What are your members? Is your uterus a member of you? Do you need crutches to walk with only one ovary?

disposal of all body fluids,

blood, amniotic fluid, shit. Tears. More blood. More tears; ours.

scraping of flesh from bones,

When scraping out the uterus lining with a curette, wait for the gritty sensation of metal against myometrial muscle. It makes the sound you would expect.

tearing eyes from the sockets,

We did that, yes, but the eyes are ovarian cysts and we delighted in our skill at shelling them out neatly. And fibroids. Neatly.

or similar terrifying manipulations.

No one was being tortured; the babies were born, the women operated on while in a deep sleep, the doctors were learning, all night.

After the novice shaman has been reduced to a skeleton

I had forgotten the ideas I had come into the program with. I was disappointed at not becoming a surgeon; I would not be permitted to be easily enraged.

the bones are covered with new flesh

I became a G.P. I took out a bank loan, I bought a desk. Fish tanks, baby fish.

and he or she receives fresh blood.

Women came to see me, asking for my hands. Men and babies and old people came in my door, they sat down and talked about themselves, they wanted me to know.

The next important stage of the shamanic journey is the ascent to the heavenly regions

The day came when I delivered Jane, and signed my name to the chart, the reward of having managed it, done it, finished it.

by means of a pole, birch tree, rainbow, or a magical flight.

There is an elevator to the fifth floor that only Staff can use. If you know the right button to push, the back door opens right into the delivery suite.

In a genuine shaman, the initiatory death is always followed by resurrection

It is born. I am born. We are born.

resolution of the crisis

This does not happen. There is an endless flow of interesting work to do. There is always a crisis but it no longer lurks behind a door marked for personnel more authorised than I.

and good integration of the experience into everyday life. Accomplished shamans have to be able to function in the ordinary world as well as or better than their fellow tribesmen.

They are not expected to stand looking out that window and thinking, but to remain active, showing neither cruelty nor pity. They are not to become demoralized.

They are good businessmen

If you have no intention of paying for our services, kindly announce this at the first interview.

practical psychologists,

There is no end to the griefs that people bring us; there is, however, an end to the working day. When we meet you on the street, we have forgotten all those secrets you told us, believe me.

masters of ceremonies,

Ceremonies I know, exulting in my secret heart as the baby is born, even as I remain smooth-browed. I know how to put the child in the father's arms. I know how to lead the relatives in to say goodbye to the corpse. I applaud the marriage, I arrange the adoption with joyful hello on one hand and sad goodbye on the other.

artists and poets, as well as healers, seers, and psychopomps.

I brought an artist to sketch the labours. She is a poet too. As for being a healer and seer, surely I can diagnose some ailments over the telephone. From listening to the spouse. From weighing the child.

They feel at home in the ordinary and nonordinary realities, can cross their thresholds at will, and are able to mediate this transition for other people.

I tell the tense businessman to meditate, the pregnant lawyer to learn Lamaze breathing. I tell the New Age mother that herbs will not protect her child from polio, that there are no nerves to the legs that can be affected by manipulating the cranium. I show poetry to surgeons and immunology texts to theosophists.

In the experiences of individuals whose transpersonal crises have strong shamanic features, there is great emphasis on personal suffering and encounter with death followed by rebirth and elements of ascent or magical flight.

I have not suffered as these poor people have suffered. For me there was no abandonment, no widowhood, no beatings, no rape, no stillbirth, no death. All these encounters I watched happen to others. They are there in my soul just the same. I needed the rebirth; every descent into the maelstrom of other people's lives requires that I ascend again into my own. At night I dream, not of flying, but of perfect births.

They also typically sense a special connection with the elements of nature

My office is filled with plants. I have no patience with wistful beliefs that plants think, hear, know us. They grow, that is enough.

and experience communication with animals or animal spirits.

Tropical fish. They grow, they reproduce. Are well known to have a calming effect on distraught people. I put the tanks on the filing cabinets. They swim regally over the facts.

it is also not unusual to feel an upsurge of extraordinary powers and impulses to heal.

It is you who have given me this; the extraordinary powers were yours. I have taken what happened to you and made it part of myself. The struggle ahead is learning how to give some of it back.

¶ *Kirsten Emmott*

LIONS, CROCODILES, AND OLD RED FOXES: THE LIVES OF PATIENTS

DANSE MARINE

riding on the flood
of desire fulfilled
into the dark cave
they wriggle
born on deep currents
to the sphere
poised
to still their swimming hordes
replete
with the embrace
of dismembered
victor
in the sexual ballet

¶ *J. Lalouette*

THE FETUS IS STOPPED AT THE BORDER

Name?
Father's name? Mother's maiden name?
Let's see your I.D. bracelet.
Same spelling?
Wait here, I'll check.
Yes, here's our file on you.
We've had you under surveillance for months.
When we didn't approve of your position
we made sure you got turned around . . .
You and your parents wait here, please.
Through there.
Let's have a listen to your heartbeat.
Doug, just listen to this heartbeat, will you?
Thanks.
O.K., fella, hold still for the electrode.
This machine will tell us the truth.
Just check this printout, will you, Doug?
Now then, fella.
Look – there's no need to get excited, to shit yourself,
just a routine medical is all . . .
You don't enter this country
without paperwork, delays . . .
How long have you been waiting? two hours?
Not long now.
We'll have you through in just a minute.
All right – here we go.
Through that door.
This way – just follow the light –
your friends are waiting.
Welcome to Canada, sir.
Drive carefully . . .

¶ *Kirsten Emmott*

LABOUR AND DELIVERY

i. *When lions are too close*

My wife and I enter
the labour and delivery room
with primal things on our minds,
in her loins,
two wildebeests more meant for the savannah,
for accomplishing the serious business of birthing
before the lions come.
But she backs up in her labour,
for the nurse is droning on
about having missed her coffee breaks
and goes about laying out on the green drape:
two vials of synthetic hormone,
two sets of surgical gloves,
an amniotomy hook,
then sixteen sets
of surgical clamps,
as though they have a clamp
for every feeling we come in with.
A heavy-duty directive
to sublimate,
to turn the natural into the man-made,
the man-brought-on.

Is this one more dig
at organized medicine?

Or are we simply
not yet ready;
have we come in too soon
to overcome that backing-up
that always happens in a hospital,

when lions are too close.

ii. *You and yours*

When you wind up with a girl
to add to the boy
you already have,
when you've accomplished that miracle
of "one of each"
in a family known for the rarity of girls;
when the labour's gone well, as smoothly
as such monumental strainings ever go;
when it's all been enjoyed by dad
at his good wife's side,
then the fact that the couple
next curtain over
in the semi-private suite
– who only speak Ukrainian well
had a baby girl with a "prolapse of the cord,"
now doing badly
in Intensive Care,
– is just another fact.
No cause to cut into your joy
except for momentary twinges
when you pass them by
on visits.

And then that thank-God reflex,
that once again the wheel of doom
has not landed on you,
or yours.

¶ *Ron Charach*

BIRTH IN INUVIK

As I fall asleep
they call me,
the midnight sun
just set

We meet
at the door
to Maternity,
her mother
in a parka
shell

A show
of blood
the pains
came on sudden
her waters broke

We are in
the birth room
her blue jeans
thrown off,
leather jacket
a rock 'n roll
skull and bones

Sixteen this summer,
silent eyes wide cheeks
black hair loose
on the pillow

Voiceless,
the big pangs
of woman years
rock through her
she takes them in

No cry
betrays her
a crease
of concentration
in her smooth forehead

Her mother,
the grandmother,
herself with a new one last year
helps at the head
of the bed

Dampens her temples
whispers strange
serious words in her ear
smiles wide and polite at me

The blue-eyed doctor
in a snow-white coat

The baby comes easy
easy as the sunrise

¶ *Robbie Newton Drummond*

24

AFTERBIRTH

If Friday's child
is so loving and giving
why is it taking so long
for the afterbirth to appear?

Plop-type delivery
on a Friday afternoon,
and now the placenta
is stuck, inside.

I wait and I wait, and I wait,
and my patients back at the office wait,
but Mother Nature has taken more than a coffee break.
The anesthetist arrives
and once the patient is put to sleep
I take a deep breath
and begin
the ascent
through vagina
beyond cervix
climbing solo
to the upper reaches of uterus,
that dark cave.
Warm blood oozes
through my surgical gown
through my skin
and into my veins.
I realize too late
that beneath my gown
I've forgotten to roll up
the right sleeve of my new shirt.

Fresh blood stains.
Only blood stains.

Abruptly the cervix comes to life
contracting and clamping down
on my forearm
like distempered Cerberus
at the Gate.
My muscles spasm.
I'm in deep trouble
Will I ever play racquetball again?

Where is that placenta,
that elusive pancake
with the string attached?
The bloody tide turns.
I've got it.
In a flash
it's in the pan:
glistening red and silver,
quivering creature from the deep.
My arm aches
triumphantly.

Only blood remains.
Only blood stains.

¶ *Vincent Hanlon*

THE OBSTETRICAL PATTER (*When Magic Fails*)

After a handful of days and nights
in the delivery room
I soon master the obstetrical patter:
"Push into your bum"
"It won't be long now"
"You're doing very well"
"With the next contraction
you'll have your baby."
A good script
and a natural delivery
make all the difference.
Besides, there are only so many things
one can say
to a woman about to give birth.

It's an exciting time.
Coax the head out ever so slowly,
then free the shoulders,
one, then the other.
Things are picking up speed now,
a flash of back, bum, and legs, feet.
No fumbling here
only a well-executed flourish
as the baby is guided
in a graceful arc up
onto the mother's flattened abdomen.
"A beautiful boy!"
The exclamation is sung
on a note of triumph.
Here, under the bright lights,
giving birth,
performing the miracle of life,
this holy place is where I belong.

Or at least, so I felt,
until the evening my magic failed.
At first, I was so preoccupied
with my sparkling sleight of hand
I failed to see what happened.
The audience is noticeably subdued.
Where is the usual joyful hysteria?
"He has Down's Syndrome," she says, puzzled.

As I look at the baby
then at the mother
my mind scrambles for a reply
this isn't supposed to happen
to mothers under thirty-five
I'm thinking.
She interrupts my thoughts,
"My baby has Down's Syndrome,"
she says quietly, simply,
to no one in particular.
"Yes," I reply, as quietly,
and look at my hands.

¶ *Vincent Hanlon*

CHRISTMAS DELIVERY

This is a discharge summary
on patient, Mary, hospital record #251200
admitted on 25 December.
Patient was admitted to case room
in early labour.
Husband, Joseph,
sent downstairs to admitting office
to sign forms.
Patient seen and examined.
21 year old, first pregnancy;
Last Menstrual Period: 20 March;
Estimated Date of Confinement: 25 December.
No significant past medical history. Period.
Patient's vital signs stable.
Cervix 2 centimetres dilated;
Vertex presentation.

As the patient began to mind contractions
she asked for something for pain.
Intramuscular injection of Demerol was given with good relief.
Spontaneous rupture of membranes.
Copious amounts of blood-stained amniotic fluid.
Strong contractions every 3-4 minutes.
Fetal heart rate steady at 140.

Patient complained of pressure in rectum
at which time she was re-examined.
Somewhat surprisingly cervix fully dilated.
Patient, accompanied by husband,
transferred to delivery room.
Patient was instructed by nurse:
When you feel a contraction coming on
take a deep breath and hold it.
You're having a contraction now.
Push, push, push, PUSH,
Push into your bottom Mary.

There, that's it.
You're doing fine.
Look in the mirror:
See the baby's hair, Mary.
Another big breath now.
Come on Mary, push, push, PUSH.

Perineum anesthetized;
Midline episiotomy cut.
Controlled vaginal delivery
of healthy male Christ child.
He cried spontaneously.
Cord clamped, and cut by a somewhat apprehensive father.

Episiotomy repaired.
Estimated blood loss: 300 millilitres.
Infant examined: no abnormality detected.
Patient and spouse congratulated.
Mother and father encouraged by nurse
to spend a few minutes bonding with infant.
Breast feeding attempted.
Patient transferred to recovery room.
Infant transferred to newborn nursery.
Afterward, according to the nurse's notes,
Mary kept all these things,
and pondered them in her heart.
End of dictation. Thanks very much.

¶ *Vincent Hanlon*

MY SON

Shadow of my dreams,
dream of my awakening.
Your deathless dance
traces with grace my halting, guilty steps –
I try to shed your specter,
> flee you
> outrun you
> but I only catch you,
> embrace you in my hot tears
> with my arms full of –
> nothing.
How long is the gestation of a dream?
> a dream never born,
> a dream unthinkingly torn,
> from the womb that has grown closed
> waiting for your birth?

Your seventeen year old shadow
now towers over mine.
Unlike other teenagers,
I can put the words in your mouth,
the talent in your brain and hand,
but the animation I will on you
is a cartoon,
a chimera, and no more.

Can you not hold still long enough
for me to tell you
I loved you?   I love you still!
It is sarcasm that I hear in your laughter now,
Where once were baby tears?
Tears I could not brush away,
hush away in a mother's embrace?

Yet I am a mother, one with all mothers.
I will always have a fragment of you within me,
hold close the memories that weren't
remember the little hands that didn't
I am your mother still.

¶ *Ariel Boilen*

A HOSPITAL FOR SICK CHILDREN

This is a hospital for sick
children.
They walk the rooms,
wards and halls,
each one
a testimony to
tragedy's
greater or lesser thrall.

The bald-headed ones
of all ages and sizes
with hat or scarf
to cover up the mark
of their struggle;
with teddy bears,
ice cream,
the usual paraphernalia
of childhood.

And the little ones
strangely alone
in this vast metropolis
of unfamiliar faces
crying in a crib in the
corridor.

The parents waiting
room,
accumulating a pall
of anguish
that hangs like smoke
in a Friday night bar.
The endless wait
for news, hours
on end,
silent sitting,
lying, smoking,
drinking
coffee.

Sometimes
the agony broken
by a green-suited man
explaining his craft
to a couple
benumbed by shock
or relief.

The parents no longer seen,
in a nightmare
of waiting by
the bedside
with incredible grief
or terrible acceptance.

When I come in
I say a prayer
to a God I don't
believe in that
my children will
never need me
here.

¶ *Heather Weir*

NURSERY

Busy afternoon schedule,
Interrupted
By the piercing squeal of a pocket beeper.
The summons, urgently, to the nursery
"Please come and intubate a baby."
Left behind,
Two fractured noses, and a case
Of tonsillitis
That any idiot with an x-ray and a prescription pad
Could treat.
I'm off to intubate a baby
In the nursery.

No elevator.
Damn things stop automatically
The minute you push the call button.
Visions of blue babies.
I race up six flights of stairs.
Out of shape, myself nearly blue
I sprint into the nursery.
"Where's the baby?" Gasping.
"Should have called me STAT!"

Staff neonatologist by the x-ray viewer
Doesn't quite smile.
"No need to run.
Come look at the x-ray first."
My God.
Bilateral pneumothoraces.
Staggering, to the incubator.

There he lies.
Twenty-six-week preemie
Glistening translucent skin with spiderweb veins
No longer pink
With the glow of young life.
Mottled now,
White and yellow,
Livid blue.
No respirator tube.
No movement.

"When?"
"About an hour ago."
So calm she is.
The professional, the doctor.
I sense the hurt beneath her face, serene.
It always hurts to lose one.
"He was doing so well . . ."

I practice. We all do.
All five of us, four interns, one student.
Extend neck. Laryngoscope in.
Lift.
Look.
Slide the tube in, so.
Now bag. Watch the chest for movement. Listen.
The body is still warm, from the incubator.
Still warm and supple. So lifelike
But not alive.
Tiny eggshell skull, cupped in my hand.
He only lived one day.

Yet even such a brief life can have purpose.
To teach, to demonstrate.
We learn.

Maybe next time.

¶ *M.A. Bramstrup*

HOSPITALIZED CHILD

The little child
with pleading eyes
sees "father"
in my warm hand.

The honks and whistles
in the street,
the TV's blinking dots,
cries and laughs and a rolling ball
are all cut loose,
as a thoughtlessly
gliding palm
and a gentle poke
from a roving finger
finally
find the spot.

¶ *Daniel Lowe*

BEGINNING THE THAW

"Little Eddie's feet were so damn cold
he couldn't hardly feel them
when they drove him to the hospital.
Little bugger – who can keep an eye
on a kid like that,
he's into everything; how'd I know
he left without no rubbers on?
It's enough I got homework t'do,
fourth time in grade three
and they all call me dumb-dumb; not so dumb
like Eddie, though;
I know how cold it gets out there.
Doc at the Children's said Eddie's toes
might have t'come off;
maybe on one foot, maybe both;
they turned blue and now they're black.
Eddie di'n't seem to care;
just laughin' and cryin' all the way down,
at the way them toes were ticklin' him
when they begin to thaw."

¶ *Ron Charach*

COME UP TO THE CRIB

Wizened little men come to see
the blue-red babe;
fresh off the burn ward
their faces like washed leather,
scowling like little Frankensteins.

Baby closes out the sight of them;
somewhere else, escapes
through her scalp holes
and up the tubes like Alice.

What colour are the bugs in an Indian lung.

In the blue-tiled room
little zombies come up to the crib
to find the untouchable doll.

¶ *Ron Charach*

PUMPKINHEAD

when I pass by
in the glass corridor
you jump up to scare me,
great-big mouthful of teeth and a bright-orange head
of iodine

Surprise! the kid can't walk any more,
but she c'n jump at needle-time –

scalp as thick as a basket by now;
seventy wire stitches
to let out one bad bit of extra brain

that wasn't thinking anyway

¶ *Ron Charach*

FAILURE TO THRIVE

We wish there was only one way to fail,
a hapless babe or two
lacking the know-how
to drink, breathe and swallow
at the same time.

Instead of this progeny of souls
who received no love,
so can give none;
legions of near-retarded moms on welfare
with a drunken father on a parkbench
as a template,
and an ex-con boyfriend
who likes his women fat
and afraid.

They cannot heat bottles,
they clutch at cigarette logjams
and drown in a sea of beer
the truck discharges at their door.
And if they water down baby's formula,
it's because "everybody has to make do";
baby's developing brain too.

Elvis, belt that corny line again:
   "He'll grow to be an angry young man
   some day . . ."
He'll break his mammy's heart
his sweetheart's jaw
and some kind of record
for putting fists through walls.

For now
we notify the Authorities
when the lonely little mother fails
to show for the follow-up

Oh, you sunken-eyed kid
with the big round head
and the "preemie look"
pulled so early from the promised land
of infancy,
one wintry night of early darkness
I saw your nurse come alive,
no, *thrive*,
when you finally kept down
all your feeds,
and your great big eyes
started shining.

¶ *Ron Charach*

INTENSIVE CARE

(for Patrick, 12 months old)

There is a Buddha
in this small yellow body,
with the bean head
and hands, smaller than a spider monkey's

Bones, frail as a slender smile
feet curl to lotus petals
eyes, wise and bright
with jaundice and injections,

He knows

Ageless, elusive as incense
his gaze cuts me to the quick
before words, he will be
dead

¶ *Robbie Newton Drummond*

CANCER OF THE BLOOD

The boy is in the private room
sheets tucked up to his ears
white blood jumbled inside
his arteries. The marrow succumbs
to anarchy. Stray cells wander
through the walls of defense. The enemy
camps like squatting gypsies
in the suburbs of his body's flesh.

The boy, still high
in the tree of his first
thousand apple barrel runs,
cannot control the break-
down of the code the unimaginable
code of his genes where generals
churn out strange gibberish,
the secretaries of state type up
queer memos the big machinery moves
and the infantry charges aimlessly over
the brink. His blood runs foul
with warboats and weird contraptions
meant to mangle and maim.

He cannot stop
to pick up the stray
cat in the neighbour's yard
or play wooden guns and soldiers
with the boys on his block
waiting for his Dad to come home
from work in the coal mines.
A nuclear war goes off in the high
crest of his pelvis and the walls
fall to the trumpets
of an old Jericho.

¶ *Robbie Newton Drummond*

SHE WAS A REFRACTORY CHILD

She had a doll she found
in a vacant lot, its head split
　　open
its left leg burned
　　off
she wouldn't throw it
　　out.

¶ *Arthur Clark*

STEPHANIE

She was smart
poised
in the invincible shield
of her youth
worldwise
bulletproof.

(They found her sprawled across the sheets
  limbs flung doll-like on the bed
one arm dangled to an open bottle
  blue-and-orange capsules.)

She was into Def Leppard
Guns 'N' Roses
Patrick Swayze and Dirty Dancing.
She cared about acid rain
nuclear war, Amazon rainforest.

(Her hospital gown once pressed and clean
  now black-stained with liquid charcoal
yellowgreen vomitus sloshed in a basin
  where pill fragments glistened.)

And yet
crises at home
tension at school.
Pressure and stress
wrenched her innards
undertow of panic
crosscurrents of fear.

(Greased tube curved worm-like
  through the portal of her nostril
monitor leads like thin tentacles
  curled across her chest.)

Her friends wouldn't care.
Her parents wouldn't understand.
She just knew it.
She made the call
only to be met
by the metallic voice
of a tape-recorded message
aloof, dispassionate.
It was the last thing
she needed to hear.

(Friends, parents waited
   in a dimly lit room
faces cupped in anxious hands.
   Thin carpets absorbed their sighs
as they leaned against
   the silent walls.)

Her body squirmed
her limbs tossed
as she recovered.
She woke up
to a half-circle of faces.

She looked around
and smiled
and closed her eyes.
She would talk when she was ready.

¶ *Gerry Greenstone*

WHITE LACES

"I'm not going to start any fights
unless somebody else does."

He's only 15, but looks older,
weathered, in an inked-on bluejean jacket,
his blueberry Doc Martins spanking new,
scissor-botched hair, but good-looking
in a James Dean way, but
intelligence: average. potential: almost average.
And he just can't get too keen.

Admits he's a target
for the cops – "The Beast" –
or any rival gang that happens to be out –
"White laces means White supremacy"
(were these calf-high risers once a polio shoe?)

Says it's worse in the wintertime
when the snow turns to grey slush
and everybody's freezing their nuts off,
and down, and just looking for someone
to take it out on.

How can he just walk away from the street
when all his friends
(each more fatherless
than the next)
run with gangs.
Skinheads in Mohawks
Mods with the checkered sash,
B-Boys in oversize hats and black skins,
all combing the city streets,
not one with a plan
for tackling this week's
homework.

Easy for me to say settle down.
He knows all the Metros by their first names
and they know him.
He was there at the Ex on Black Sunday
when they bowled over everyone
and ran off with a thousand bucksworth
of stuffed animals.

"I can't just go out and buy new friends
at the Eaton Center,
now can I, Doc?"

Downplays his knack
for finding instant brothers.

¶ *Ron Charach*

SNAKE

"Edna, Judy, Harley, Eric or Marjorie,
Meet the long snake. Thinner than a garden hose
thicker than a strand of spaghetti. Firmer than *al dente*
and, oh yes, we need to remove
your false teeth.

"We're going to wash out some of those pills.
It's easier than it looks.
The secret is to relax.
Relax, don't panic, and swallow,
swallow, and swallow some more.
You're forgetting to breathe
through your nose.

"If you feel the urge to vomit, Do.
Up the tube, or around the tube,
it doesn't really matter.
Spit it all out. That's it.
Spit out all that nastiness.

"We're doing the washing now.
Rinse, rinse, and one final rinse.
You're doing fine.
Almost finished.
We'll clean you up soon."

Homestretch.
Down goes the charcoal.
Black, black, very black.

The long black snake
slips gracefully up
the dark passageway
and out of the mouth.

My gaze shifts from
the dripping tail of the snake
to the floor.
My feet.
I am suddenly aware
that no vomit or charcoal
have splashed on my new
and comfortable sandals.

¶ *Vincent Hanlon*

A LOVER'S QUARREL

Describe it simply
as a lovers' quarrel
after which she slashed her wrist
and sought medical attention.

A superficial laceration
over the right wrist.
No active bleeding.
Clean the area with antiseptic
and pick away the dried clot.
Tidy tidy.
A scratch on the skin
parallels the main cut:
presumably an initial
tentative testing of the flesh.
Don't look here
for the confident opening incision
or a surgeon amputating a limb.
Instead, observe the hesitant and unsuccessful
pruning of the hand that caresses.

What is a doctor to do?
So late at night.
First of all, be gentle with the tissues.
Restore the natural anatomy
with a close approximation of the skin edges.
Use a small needle.
Minimize the small talk.

"You are very brave,"
she says when we're finished.
I don't argue.
It's too early in the morning
to start another lovers' quarrel.

¶ *Vincent Hanlon*

RUBBERS AND FOAM

"Rubbers and foam."
Her answer is nonchalant
as "toast and jam."
She's fourteen,
"almost fifteen," she adds,
"and I want to switch over to the Pill."
She and her boyfriend of six months
don't want to take any more chances,
no matter how small.
"And yes, as a matter of fact,
I have discussed the whole thing
with my mother.
My dad, well,
he's not quite ready yet."

But she's ready.
The whole world lies naked in her bed
and almost everything is under control.
She has all the self-assurance
of a Cosmo girl
or an actress in a tampon ad.

I pretend to treat her
like a woman –
A few words about pap tests,
breast exams,
VD,
cigarettes.
If you're old enough to smoke
in bed,
you're old enough to stay as healthy
as you can.

She pretends to be hearing these things
for the first time.
And she does have a question for me:
"Can you get Herpes more than once?"
So I tell her a few things about Herpes.
She agrees to check back in two months,
sooner if anything goes wrong.
Somehow that seems unlikely.

¶ *Vincent Hanlon*

THE SLIM

The lover is thin
starved to a minor key.
The lover has black circles for eyes.
He has been in the underbelly.
He cracked the egg in his smooth palm,
the albumin ran clear beneath the yolk.
A little blue flame of happiness quivered.
He licked in with the pulse of capillaries.
In a blush of arousal the devil of moments
had him by the short hairs. The deep blue
sea sent no bubble of fear.

The slim cajole him into their ranks.
A new soldier joins the slender column.

Below the day's glad vapours it is dark.
A connection is made, the fix
of bliss, the slow wash of the moment.
Everyman strips off his pinstripe
and is naked as a young lover a young
lover in a boat without oars.

Above us the tower of babel
swells. The towers of glass lift
their impervious skin. Slim crept in
through the basement door,
the plague of crumbles crept in.

Slim Jim
lies in the cool of his bed
amidst the potions and contraptions.
The sisters of succour in white
habits attend his diminishing.
Look close, fellow beings
he is not the doomed youth
the evil boy, the addict of moments
the whore-girl, he is our brother
drawn slim by an ancient fact . . .
World corrupts Everyman. It rots,
dear mortal, it rots. The disease
of the white blood is the new disease
of the old fall. The bright angel of fire
in a red plume long as the millenia
falls from Grace.

¶ *Robbie Newton Drummond*

THE SPIRITS FUNNEL

Each fatty infiltration,
each Laennec cirrhosis
tells of a life history of crying
of one kind or another,
whether it takes place in a hamlet of Calabria,
on a Harlem street
or small village below
the Karavanke mountains;
businessmen lunchers
and Bay Street lawyers
not excepted.

How often do you hear,
"No, Doc, I don't drink alcohol."
But by now you know such innocence
does not exclude a case of beer,
two litres of home-made wine
or a bottle of vodka a day . . .

"Please, make my husband
to quit booze,
but don't let on I tell you!"
Don't be annoyed with her,
just desperate hypocrisy
born out of years
of being battered.

Every new research paper
makes you feel more disappointed
with your efforts to loosen
the devil's embrace.
A.A., Donwood Institute?
"Cummon, Doc, I'm certainly not
one of *those*. I'd much prefer
to quit on my own."

Paresthesiae and weakness,
indigestion, hematemesis,
tremor and impotence,
and the unpredictable incontinence
– a compendium of scientific terms.
"Why, Doc, can't you send me to a specialist?
There must be something else wrong!"
The most painstaking disease to treat,
the one that frustrates
repeatedly –

And all the ambivalent thoughts:
You wish his foreman
would finally find out
– but what if the threat of losing his job
is not a deterrent at all,
but pushes him further
into humiliation?

He asks for a note
for a few days off; will he rest,
or imbibe unrestrictedly?

I bow this sobered head
to every son of an alcoholic
who somehow manages to pull himself up
through the spirits funnel.

¶ *Mladen Seidl*

Hell
       if it ain't
ol' Uncle Jarrod
              & his DT's
       headfirst
              in the flowerbed
       shoulders shrugged,

       Through all the
early hours
       he trembled
              the half moon
                     with Quakey the knee
       and Flubber the lips
              & now Uncle Stubble with the shoes
is flat out, deep in the drink of dreams
       on Papa's carpet lawn
       this dawning
              even Dog ain't
       bitin'
at the bait

       Ma woulda said
       "bring 'im in"
fed him flapjacks 'n
       instant coffee . . .
       Ma's dead a shakes
       these past ten years
hard spirits'll
       have to do

I'd shout out
"wake up, wake up!"
 but that'd only scare away
 the sparrows . . .
drink little sparrows
 in the marble bath
  a body's length from
ol' Jarrod
    the drunk
  I think not even rain'd
  touch 'im today

¶ *Robbie Newton Drummond*

THICK HONEY

When a man in his grey beard gives way
to the thick honey of strong drink
when his son with the new bones the tall bones
when he sees his old man down on the floor
when he hears how his words
fall like daubs of soft lead
when a boy sees his old man his mother's man
when he sees him stumble and just stand
when he sees him small like a man in a cap

When a man takes his new man his tall boy
when a man in his dirty clothes
when a man in his sneakers takes his son aside
and opens a fist on his scattered change and says
"splay me a quarter's worth, lay me a round"
when a son sees his father in a slurry of haze

When a father and son see the dawn break
when the sun lurches into the sky
and the blue is new as an old coat
when a father says "son I gotta tell you"
when a son says "nuts dad me and the boys . . ."
when they both come stinking into the yard
and the chickens scramble and the dogs whine
and the door is locked when it so happens
that the door is locked and in the kitchen
the mother kneads a bitter bread
and ties the sheaves in knotted thread

Then
we will have brotherhood
amongst the fallen
like trees
in a landslide

¶ *Robbie Newton Drummond*

SUICIDE

A bullet meant for a yearling moose
finds a home behind the chin of Evans Day
neat hole, the back of his head blown off
downriver at his old man's fish camp
his music machine still winds out
the music of the far south rhythm and blues
guitar riffs full of the chaos of culture
in the photograph above his mother's bed
Niagara Falls seduces with its white veils
like the promise of a gameshow honeymoon

No, Evans
you did not get your chance
to come over the falls with us
like a daredevil barrel man
inviting gravity with fog
to join us at the bottom
by the Maiden Of The Mist
we fell over the brim
before we were born
we live in a bridal suite
with doorprizes and two new cars
in an atheism of ideas
glittering gaudy hollow

Evans, with the Inuvialuit name
Sik Sik, the ground squirrel
you could not make the flight
over the falls into our gay
and sordid wedding feast
you did the next best thing
you killed your yellow sun
in the big north sky
with a beer drunk bullet
congratulations!

¶ *Robbie Newton Drummond*

LOOKING FOR EXTRA HANDS

They wear long black mats of bloodied hair
bluejean jackets under the soaked-through gowns;
they have a thick fruity smell
and come in tied to stretchers,
their faces puffy at 4 a.m.

At least Johnny Wapamoose
screaming for the Doc,
his restraints growing thinner;

Nothing near weighs more than the water tap;
I try to smile, and look for extra hands

Tomorrow, sober,
he'll lie still enough on the ward,
his first good meal in months.

¶ *Ron Charach*

EQUIPOISE (*How Big, How Cut, and How Hard*)

"It's a veterinary steroid
used with horses, pigs and dogs;
I myself don't take it
because it blows you up
like a balloon.
It also gives you bitch's teats,
then you have to go get lipo-
suction
to get them off your pec's;
they *hurt*.

But you got to take *something*
Dianabol,
Methandrostenelone,
or better, one that's not
a testosterone (too many side effects).
Because in the end what counts
is how big, how cut
and how hard you are.
Schwarzenegger takes them,
Everybody knows it,
and Ben Johnson uses
growth hormone –
All the Olympians take them,
They nearly had to cancel a Pan Am Games
because 9 of the athletes tested positive
and 17 others packed their bags and went home
just so they wouldn't have to be
tested.
All the Big Boys take them,
– *You* even take them – Whaddayou *think*,
Don't you still eat chicken
or beef? They're nothing
but thin skin
over chemical
muscle."

¶ *Ron Charach*

JUNKIE ON THE PHONE

You don't have a headache.
The GP you named doesn't know you.
The pharmacist recognizes your name.
You even called *me* before.
I won't prescribe the drugs.
Play the game elsewhere.
Call up some other doctor.
Set out your lies:
"Doctor, here is my lie.
I want you to join in my lying.
Pretend I am sick.
Give me what will make me sicker.
Give me a stick
with which to beat myself.
Help me to die."

¶ *Kirsten Emmott*

A MEMORABLE STORY

It was a memorable story,
full of vivid details.
You told it well.
First the car crash
two years ago
the still unforgettable image
of your wife
hurtling through the rear window
onto the dark and lifeless pavement.
Since then your skull-splitting headaches
the nausea, the darkened room
the cool washcloth
brought to you
by your motherless son.
And what a son,
only eight years old,
already speaking three languages,
taught by his Chinese nanny
and his sister's French nanny.
For you are, incidentally,
a man of some wealth,
painfully rich after the car insurance
and courageous in your devotion
to the children.
Kids and nannies travel with you
on long assignments to the Arctic
(notice the little t-shirt from Resolute Bay)
where migraine headaches are a constant threat;
no consolation but the Northern Lights
and a few extra pills in your pocket.

It was a good story,
a sad story,
of modest heroism in the face of adversity,
the significance
only now apparent.
For such a story
I willingly exchanged a prescription
for tablets containing
your favourite narcotic,
your warm moist handshake
and the memorable promise
of a polar bear rug
in six months time.

¶ *Vincent Hanlon*

A LOVER'S PRAYER (*SCHIZOPHRENIA*)

This is me. This is not all of me
The rest is trapped behind
a divorcing glass,
through which no love
may touch or pass.

My mind takes off on frenzied trips
which pass as thought
And leaves my body here alone
deserted and distraught.

My love, I pray that some small part
remain
to bring the rest of me
to you again.

¶ *Betty Ujanen*

DIFFERENCES

First it was my father
And then my mother too,
And when they convinced my brothers,
The place became a zoo.

They called in Dr Patterson,
and I overheard him say:
"This time we must do something,
He can't go on this way."

  (But this way is my way,
  This way is me.
  And if I'm not like others,
  Why can't they let me be?)

They took me to the hospital,
And for the first time I was scared.
A bunch of doctors asked me things,
But I didn't think they cared.

They said that I was suffering
from a disease which split the mind,
And they put me in an airless room
With others of my kind.

  (But this way's *not* my way,
  This way's not me.
  I've never hurt another soul;
  Why can't they let me be?)

The doctor said it wouldn't hurt
That the treatments caused no harm.
And they put me on a stretcher,
And put a needle in my arm.

And then when I was floating,
I heard this voice which said:
"You two hold down the body,
And I'll hold down the head."
I don't remember very much
Of the things which happened then.
I guess I grew less crazy,
And men became just men.

The castles all came tumbling down,
And the prince refused to grieve,
And the female essence ebbed away,
So they gave me weekend leave.

The doctor said it won't be long
Before I can go home,
And for some unknown reason
I feel so much alone,
As though I've lost a melody
I can't quite bring to mind,
With fragments of an old refrain
Of an entirely different kind.

¶ *Robert W. Shepherd*

INTERNAL BLEEDING

Memories of The Man
  return sharp and clear
  his strong hands
  playing upon your skin.
He stripped away
  your childhood
  and forced you
  into the hot humid world
  of adult need.

He kept you silent
  with threats
  but with affection too.
A man with
  a child's pain
  stirring confusion
  in a young boy's mind.

You blamed
  your parents
  whose fault
  wasn't collusion
  but failure
  to hear the tremor
  in your voice
  or read the anguish
  in your eyes.

Troubles at school
  arguments at home
  whitehot rage
  in your chest.
Shame, disgust
  congealed
  deep inside the gut
  where nothing could reach.

Peers sensed
   something simmering
   just inside the skin.
Your confusion
   caused discomfort;
   it was catchy; they turned away
   which only proved
   you were worthless.

Years later
   it erupted
   in clarity
   when they found you
   under the stairs
   with a younger boy.

Teachers, counsellors
   doctors, parents
   all shook their heads
   wondering why
   it took them so long.

Let there be a place
   where you will feel
   the hurting stop,
   the healing begin.

¶ *Gerry Greenstone*

WHY NOT TRY AN IGUANA

I saw you on the windy street, standing
before the straw in the smokey window,
choosing a pet with no one to guide you.
Once you could have buttonholed the manager
insisting that he speculate
about travel in the 90's,
poking his chest as you backed him up
towards the belt;
gone. your inheritance, your springs,
your good looks sucked into your vacated eyes.
you look like a motel.

At times I see you
and I cross the street;
I miss the New York cover,
a thousand immigrants per square foot,
identical in height, everyone's psychosis
worth the last seat on the subway.
What are you doing, still in your home-town,
everyone's favorite thank-God-it-wasn't-me;
and why bring your empty room the colourful bird
you could never entertain; why not try
an iguana to look down on, or

tarantulas,
to memorize –

¶ *Ron Charach*

THE MOST SERIOUS MOMENT OF OUR LIVES

Years later as Mindy's functions
began unravelling,
and she'd roll on the hospital floor
whenever she failed to get her way,
her second drink of lye
impressing not one soul
in her exhausted family.
They all agreed to
"plug her into the wall"
if the fourth and final round of pills
didn't work.
"Just wheel her back when you're finished
with her, please."
her head turned over on its side
so she can't breathe vomit,
= no aspiration.

But when her eyes unsealed in the white tile room,
and she hoarsely called for water,
she recognized my role in this,
my professional ring through the plastic.
She may have seen a liar straining
to escape from my face.
Because instead of asking about her husband
and the kids,
and who knew,
and did everybody know,
Instead she turned her electric breath on me.
Automatically I told her, "Shhh, It's O.K. now . . ."
but she looked me up and down and said "This
is the most important moment
of *our* lives."

¶ *Ron Charach*

THE WALKING WOMAN

"Ambulatory!"
That's Elaine.
She ambulates – in snow, in rain:
Flinging her arms like some élite
Regiment, to the thund'ring beat
Of drums and cymbals in the brain,
Elaine parades up Urban Street.

Oh, hear her sing!
Oh, hear her swear!
Her participles curl your hair.
She joins, in telepathic mirth,
With UFOs in the upper air
Elaine, Ambassador of Earth.

Of course, her name is not "Elaine."
She is the Princess Almondine;
Child-Goddess of the Silver Screen,
Protegée of a Billionaire.
High Fashion Model, Mafia Moll,
World-renowned Spy and Citrus Queen.

In spite of a petition, spread
By merchants of the Down-Town Mall,
Elaine is not strait-jacketed.
She is not jacketed at all.

¶ *Peter Grant*

IN THE END WITH MRS R.

As the ending of my residency nears
I think of all the human woe
  I've tried to understand.
And in the end with Mrs R.
  We all missed it!
  after four years of trying!
The whole team of us knew;
  we colluded, trance-like,
  with her determination
  to be gone.
Sad sad soul she was,
  and how she kept us working.
Yet this has been a climax that fits;
  in a tidy way – a weight is gone;
  She laid her purse –
  we found it – on the sand
before she stepped into the sea.

¶ *Carl J. Rothschild*

ON MEETING MY ANALYST IN AN UNEXPECTED PLACE

A strange view
of a man
who knows me
intimately;
every nook and
cranny.

To come up
against him
here,
surprising me
with his other
existence
outside of his room
the cocoon shape
of it
broken.

He looks different.
More frail
and diffident,
even shy.

This power of a man
who has helped me
shape
my being
and self.
Who has woven his
art with
an intricate pattern
of persian hues

just for me.

How strange
to see him
among the
hurly burly
and wonder
if the thin thread
of our cloth

still holds
in this place

¶ *Heather Weir*

DIVERTICULITIS

The malt and wine are not for me.
No thanks to the surgeon
Who has warned
Don't bloody drink.

He also said, God rest *his* soul,
That exercise will make me *worse*.
(But to walk or run
Makes me feel whole)

And what about that "liquid diet"?
To drink instead of chew your food.
If something's looking good,
Don't try it.

So only sex is still allowed.
(Can't he guess that it hurts like hell?)
Still, if That is spared,
Then pain's at times forgotten.

And all is almost
Going well.

¶ *Barry Wheeler*

78

A BITTER-SWEET REMOVAL

(I'm Not Sure That I Like This)

I'm sitting lonely on this board of a bed,
Just left, disgruntled, by a grinning nurse,
To drink five litres of saline curse
Which will clean my gut to a pristine state.
(How will it go tomorrow?)

Will they find the sigmoid too inflamed
For sweet removal, or calm,
Responsive to the surgeon's touch?
The trouble is I've seen too many surgeons
Try to find sufficient length of bowel
To fill the gap that they themselves had made.
*(I really hope after all of this
I won't need a colostomy)*

Then that post-op bit
Waking up to a choke of tubing in my throat.
(And what about the pain!)

It seems to me that last time
They cut me down my back
I had all the pain I'd ever want to have
(Thank God for Pantopon)

I think I'll not enjoy the eternal wait
For my bowel to reawaken to its call,
– Those days of N.P.O., then ice-chips, water
A dreary time to live through,
(or endure)
But Thank God for cheerful visitors and friendly nurses
Who turn up just in the nick of time
(like thoughts of going home).

¶ *Barry Wheeler*

OPEN HEART SURGERY

Post-Op Note #1

Skin shaved
Chest cracked
Heart opened
Valve split
Scar forming.

Photos on request.

Post-Op Note #2

"I am the ruins of a crystal man
and there are no sentences
but only words . . ."

   – Alden Nowlan, "Five Days in Hospital"

Post-Op Note #3

In hospital as a child
I whimpered away an afternoon
worried that a spider
on the ceiling
was going to fall on me.

My thoughts were cloudy
with a mindful of numbers
less than six –
tumbling bingo balls
in a hamster's wheel –
and fuzzy assurances
that soon I would be going home.

In the movie version
of my recent hospitalization
a friend,
by day an arts consultant,
by dream a cardiovascular surgeon,
is performing open heart surgery
on me.
The moment arrives
to replace the rotten mitral valve
with a flashy tilting disc.
The scrub nurse hands him
a quart sealer
of nuts and bolts, string,
and rusty paperclips.

Sterility is not in question.
Nothing fits.
The knots slip.
My chest cavity
slowly fills with blood.

Conscious of mounting tension
in the operating theatre
I suggest they order out
for the correct part.
I am aware of time constraints
for the operation and this movie.
The ending requires rewriting.

Behind the scenes
I opt for general anaesthesia.
"Mort,
I can't seem to get
this radial line in.
Do you want to give it a whirl?"
Cut to black.

Christ
on the surgeon's left hand
at the scrub sink
methodically washes his hands.
The circulating nurse questions him
about his scrubbing method.
No one recognizes him
wearing surgical hat and mask.
They presume he is a foreign student
with an interest in open heart surgery.
He scrutinizes
the extra-corporeal circulation machine.
The operation begins.
Christ is able to identify
most of the relevant anatomy
for the surgeon.

He seems preoccupied.
(perhaps one of a billion prayers
from one of a million scattered supplicants.)
Once the heart is open
Christ's curiosity is aroused.
The surgeon repositions the lights.
Christ takes a good look inside.

"Tak me away
Tak me away
Tak me outta here
My Got my Got tak me outta here
My Got my Got you tak me outta here
I hope my Got you take me outta here
Oh my Got
I wish you take me outta here
aaaaaannnnnnhh mmmmmnmmmm ahmnmmmmmmm."

Steve is an old man
with old feet.
One is turning to pus.
He fears strange doctors
will cut off his toe.
He wants to speak
to his doctor in Tofield.
Black joke for a black toe.

Someone gave him new boots –
red gumsoles
with shiny black rubber uppers.
He doesn't ask to die with them on
only to wear them
when he takes a pee.
His foot is too painful to walk
so the nurse wheels him to the toilet –
flash of red and black
in the chrome spokes.

At night
the fear of losing his foot
gnaws away his sleep.
His voice is a dull-edged prayer
he thrusts through and through
the surrounding bed curtain:
"Tak me away
Take me away
Tak me outta here . . . ."

In the morning
riding rubber-booted to the toilet
he says to no one in particular:
"Nobody knows who's suffering but me."

Unaccountable hours later
I surface through noisy clouds
into the refrigerated sunlight
of the Cardiac Recovery Room.
"How do you feel?"
The bluntness of the question
stuns me.
There are no words yet
only a new susceptibility to tears.

A recent paper out of Stanford
blames rubber glove prints
left on the endocardium
at the time of surgery.
My eyes brim.
I blubber.
The floor is awash with my tears.
Long stemmed roses
Hallmark cards
and two copies each
of *Playboy* and *Scientific American*
float out of the recovery room.

Freeze-dried tears –
prisms suspended on forty-five centimetre
surgical sutures –
break the light.
Alden Nowlan had Hodgkin's disease
and survived.
No matter how hoarse his voice.
he wouldn't lie to someone
who's just had open heart surgery.
His signature
in a book of his poems
verifies the fine quality
of his crystal gifts.

Lead crystal is
a sharp pin wheel.
It impresses the flesh,
refracts the course of a disease,
and sings
a pure ice-blue note
into the blood.

My windows are cold crystal squares
cut from the ice in winter
and handmelted into washboard glass.
Scrub away the scars.
Tears run in the vertical grooves
softening the brown smudge of blood
and blurring the blue edge of pain.

The fifth post-operative day
is Sunday.

Things are warming up.
"O Lord, my God,
I cried out to you
and you healed me.
O Lord, you brought me up
from the nether world;
you preserved me
from among those going down
into the pit . . ."
I looked down at my chest
and see a translucent pane
of blood-stained glass
fixed over my heart.
Communion white light
penetrates this glass darkly.
Inside
40,000,000 times per year
my heart beats against the pane,
turning crystal back to sand.
Deeper inside
I slip slowly down
the tear-slick surfaces
of the mitral valve –
a funnel-shaped tunnel,
my passageway to the pit.
I clamber upwards
to the healing ridge.

¶ *Vincent Hanlon*

FEARS AROUND HER FIVE POUNDS

Did she even ask "Jesus,
what kind of headache is this!"
Months earlier a speeding police car with no lights on
ground her leg to the curb like a cat,
and now, this more effective
second line of attack:
Her brain surrendering the minor artery
but with it the Tremblay play
even all play.
Had she been fearing that time would come again
in an unmarked car?
We made dives for an explanation
before her face could fade:
the wrong health foods?
the wrong attitudes?
some lifestyle disease.
Yet, finally her weight had been average,
witnesses say there had been colour in her cheeks,
as ruddy as her once-glistening *dura mater*
when the pathologist pulled her skull away.
And when he snipped it through
to let the blood escape
it just lay there caked,
a skull within a skull
within a deathmask.

Was it foretold from the square
of her February birth,
all the fears around her five pounds
shivering in her crib.
Yet one hundred and fifteen came nowhere near
to forcing back the enemies on both sides
of her skin.
Before she is forced into the exit,
into the last five pounds,
five memories, Remember
how she'd show up at all hours
when we needed her most
to be wide-eyed
and alive.

¶ *Ron Charach*

86

TIC DOLOREUX

It seems to me a hundred years
Since first I felt the lightning pierce my face,
Became impaled on that mute agony.
From those gathering storm clouds of despair
There is no shelter –
    not in books
    not in love
    not in my soul.

Time plays his idle game with me,
Allowing my green and glorious freedom –
Before his sudden thunderbolts
Level me again
    and again,
    and again.

He holds me in his fearful trap,
A cosmic joke, an experiment in terror.
How long before she trusts again?
How many shocks before she stops
    her talking,
    eating,
    breathing?

The thunderbolts stop short
Before delivering their lethal jolt
And, spent, they leave me for a while
To gather up the sodden remains,
To patch my sundered life together,
    But ever
    with my eye
    upon the treacherous sky.

¶ *Ariel Boilen*

FOREIGN BODY

Foreign body:
something misplaced,
like a sliver in the thumb.

His thumb is red and sore
and he's sure
there's a piece of wood in it.

After the freezing kills the pain
I begin my search.
As he watches a drop of blood
grow large on his thumb nail,
he tells me of his other foreign body.

Something misplaced:
he calls it Father,
and drives long miles
over bad roads in winter
to find him
on the third floor.

"I usually arrive in time
to feed him late breakfast.
Crumbs and small bits of egg
catch in his stubble.
Breakfast over,
it's time for his shave.

I've thought of shaving him first
and then feeding him breakfast
but he's too hungry for that.

"You ever give your father a shave?
The first time I did
I was surprised
by the smoothness of his chin.
Still wrinkled, but smooth.

"You know what bothers me?
When he shits himself.
I remember him for so many years
bigger than I was,
stronger than I was.
Vigorous.
Now he does it in his bed
and doesn't even realize
the sheets are dirty.

I probe his thumb
one last time
and then abandon my search.
I can feel his pain returning.
My apology sounds
out of place.

¶ *Vincent Hanlon*

A LIFE-SAVING ENTERPRISE

Back in the office
I gently frisk patients daily
with a hand-held
tumour-detector.

In her case,
all she wanted was a check-up,
but the amazing five-fingered machine
went "beep-bop-beep"
over her right breast,
And that's how the lump was found.

Two strangers
fortuitously collide
in an examining room
littered with ragged copies
of Reader's Digest.
A great save
in modest surroundings
(the lump was cancer and successfully removed).

We smile about it later,
and congratulate each other,
celebrating our roles
in a life-saving enterprise.
We shake our fists
fearlessly
at the crab
as he scuttles
with empty claws
back to his dark corner.

¶ *Vincent Hanlon*

CA SANDRA

One cancer cell, more nervous than the rest,
Announced one day: "The man is losing weight.
Last week our numbers managed to ingest
Two thirds of everything he ate."

They told her: "We have difficulty seeing,
While cancer cells are starving everywhere,
Why this rapacious thing, this human being
Should be the object of our love and care."

Another day she pleaded: "But the man is dying!
He has too many of us to feed!
His heart will fail, his blood will stop supplying
The essential nutrients that we need!"

"Enough!" they said, "Who needs you or your sorrow?
Cancer is Growth. Divide, in Cancer's cause!
Today we own the pancreas; tomorrow
The whole man will be ours."

And so he was.

¶ *Peter Grant*

CROCODILE

Cancer is the crocodile
in the Nile of your familiar body
green and long and pale
slim with death thought
hungrier than the river
that is you

You who once ate
langoustines and cracked crab
Moroccan oranges and black chocolate
after white wine of the Loire
and wished only for cool sheets
and deep sure sleep when the Nubian
tiptoed off the pebble shore
dazzling your skin with
moonkiss and nightshade

Sleep river
the crocodile yawns in your easy flow
sleep the sleep of old Nile
the gods of death are dead
Pharaoh and his scribes are cased in glass
the pyramids have no meaning beyond
their immensity

You are an old river
you are the Nile and the crocodile
cancer is in your blood
slow and heavy as green opium
it grows like a river in flood
it grows
a sphinx face

You are an old woman
with death in your bones
you are the Nile
you are green and long and pale
slim with death thought
you are the crocodile

¶ *Robbie Newton Drummond*

TWILIGHT EXCHANGE

our parents should stop fighting us
and go peacefully if a little confused
to the nursing homes we carefully choose
to have a last home without any fuss

edible food, the doctors the best
stale urine may be the local perfume
but they can see gardens from their rooms
and all day long they're permitted to rest

oldtimers will babble with them
or to themselves off the walls
saving us from the telephone calls
and the usual visits to comfort again

our parents should gladly ascend the ramp
and close their homes without yearning
and see that we are only returning
the love that sent us to summer camp

¶ *Shel Krakofsky*

IN CORONARY CARE

He's fifty-five
and having his first heart attack.
His wife, his second,
and twenty years his junior
can't cope.
She's running into the walls.

Tonight he and I are partners
in the Coronary Care Unit.
What lingers with me
is not the molten green line
of his erratic cardiac dance,
nor the image of his wife
caroming off the walls.

What impresses me
are this man's teeth.
Crooked yellow pickets
splaying his upper lip
and distorting his half-smile.
He snoozes open-mouthed.
Nothing false here.
I detect a residue
of necrotic heart muscle
on his foul-smelling breath.
He exhales over his raw meat tongue
and the vapours condense
on his irregularly protruding teeth.

Grey moss stains the enamel
and sticks in the cracks.
The nurse will eventually produce a toothbrush.
When he wakes
he reaches over to his bedside table;
he picks up a green apple
from the ever-present bowl of fruit.
Then he looks over at me for approval.
His bite is unique.
Those crooked dirty teeth
with which he continues to nibble away
at life's banquet.

¶ *Vincent Hanlon*

94

A CURE FOR OLD AGE

Bible reader
but no church-goer,
she became impatient
with too much ritual.
On Holy Thursday
she refused her bed bath.
The nurses were puzzled.
She deliberately mis-heard
"Bum Sunday" for "Palm Sunday"
and waved away the hot cross bun.
She feared a conspiracy
of cinnamon and lemon-icing crosses
too sweet to bear.

She is 77 years old,
she is rapidly approaching
the end of her life
and she would like no surprises.

So
what is your diagnosis,
young doctor?
Some vague toothed thing
in my belly
eating me up?
No.
I believe it's my lungs.
They first betrayed me
when I was a child.
Chronic disease of slime in the lungs,
the doctors said.
And if I could spit
spit, spit, spit it all away,
I'm sure I would feel better.

Kick,
my life has no kick.
Surely you with your silver tongue
and your skills
and your sincerity
surely you
can put the kick
back into my life.

Stop all your poking around,
young doctor.
Life ebbs.
Why not be my friend
for the rest of my days?

¶ *Vincent Hanlon*

ROUND AND DOWN

	SMALL
LOVED?	HELPLESS
CHANGED WITH DISGUST	HOSPITAL
SOILED DIAPER	BEAUTIFUL
HELPLESS, BURDEN	POTENTIAL
HOSPITAL	LOVED
FRAIL	SOILED DIAPER
FORGETFUL	CHANGED WITH JOY
OLDER	LOVED
LOVE	GROWTH
PROUD	LEARNING
FAMILY	COMPANION
ACHIEVEMENTS	

¶ *Joe Wiatrowski*

OLD FOX

He lives two lives, this old red fox
still caught in the lovely trap of youth,
confesses his dwindling flame
only when he needs me to stoke the coals
I cannot force into the forest fire he craves.

He has become a caricature of himself,
the skin lying in a cowl about his ears
entranced, he chops away the days
seeking a simpler time now fled.

As wood chips fly he dreams a dream
of mighty woods where he lived free
unfettered by a balking heart
undisputed master of his destiny.

He calls me Doc and begs for dignity
now caught in the net of years and aging flesh.
Proud tears spring to our eyes at the injustice
and he begs me to help him outfox eternity.

¶ *Ariel Boilen*

HOUSE CALL

(Where the Road of Mainland Ends)

The green grass has unknowingly
left him
as of late autumn in the jaw of December
with nothing
but dried bones and papyrus skin:

Mr Woods is 92 years old.

His eyes deep in their own chambers
refuse the swallow
of the general darkness,

faintly signal a mind that can no longer tell
his own beginnings
nor where the road of Mainland ends.

I listen to his heart and ponder:
God must have lived with him sometime
and unknowingly left.

¶ *Elmer Abear*

THE LONG ROAD TO THE SEA

There is no society
for the one who watches himself
slipping, who says – I am not what I was,
and will be less-still.
No man takes the long road to the sea
without smelling salt miles and miles ahead –
of a plunge? a striding in? an embracing
of the clear-blue water in two spotted hands,
in a senile smile that says –
Let the sea expand;
water will be water.
Even roads not taken head seaward like thirsty dogs;
and the man who never knew to learn a single stroke
gets the same
Olympic treatment.

¶ *Ron Charach*

LIFE IN THE LATE HOURS:
THE LIVES OF DOCTORS

THE FIRST CRY

It's 15 years since I first heard that cry,
yet it still echoes within me.
The culmination of a life's work,
worth all the hardship and toil.
Though it ends in sterile drapes and masks and sweat
as faceless figures mill about.

To be part of such a scene,
When, almost ready to surrender,
She reaches deep within and gives forth
one last burst of energy,
as if ready to explode.
I place myself in readiness,
feel spectator, not participant.
Then comes a cry, at first
as if far off

A child is placed upon its mother's chest,
it utters all the anticipated sounds,
after what appeared eternity.

With tears of joy
the new-found parents disappear within themselves
in quiet celebration of the miracle.
I quietly retreat, remove the blood-stained blues
and return to the bed
which hours before I left
in darkened silence.

I'll miss those cries,
the many hundred cries I've been a part of.
They've taken me to untold heights,
and filled me with the worst fears.
They've been a daily part of me.
But now it's time for change.

Perhaps I'll sleep more soundly now.
No calls to jolt me from my dreams.
I'll watch the children as they grow away,
but remember,
always,
the first cry.

¶ *H.J. Goldstein*

BACK INTO IT

In med school it was easier
  To remain detached
  To not get too involved
  With all the sad stories, the personal traumas
    That come through the door.

In those days we were
  Hooked on competitive thirst
    Stung with academic zeal
      Caught in the excitement
  Of the diagnostic puzzle
    And the therapeutic trial.

There was no time
  For doubt on an x-ray image
There was no room
  For fear on a microscope slide.

It's harder now to stay removed
  From the pained and depressed
    The bruised and jaundiced
      The anxious and bereaved
  Who reach out
    Across my desk.

But then I shake off these thoughts
  I dig in and get to work –
Eliciting signs and symptoms
  Seeking diagnostic clues
    Selecting treatment plans –
  I'm quite pleased
    With my efficiency
When freed from distraction.

But just a glance of those trouble eyes
  Or the sound of that anguished voice
    And I know in a moment
  I'm drawn back
    Into it.

¶ *Gerry Greenstone*

IT TAKES ALL SORTS

It takes all sorts,
two rows of half-propped,
nicely scrubbed,
freshly tucked,
newly panned patients;
Might be a junior nurse's paradise.
But anyone else's nightmare.
Not least the Intern's.
He wants them different as snowflakes,
needs them that way for experience:
   To sound their murmurs,
     tap their tums,
   Feel their lumps
     and prick their thumbs,
   Write histories
     like fairy tales,
   Draw blood in tubes
     as deep as pails,
   Fill forms (ink flows
     as free as wine)
   Prescribe, record, inject, suspect . . .
   And sleep betimes
     between the midnight fractured skull,
     the one o'clock appendix,
     the two o'clock strangulated hernia,
     the three o'clock suicide,
     the four o'clock coma
     (still undiagnosed)
     the five o'clock amnesia,
     the six o'clock coronary,
     the seven o'clock school bus crash

   And the eight o'clock
     bacon and eggs.

Nor any less the Resident.
He wants them puzzles, problems all.
Subtle enough for a fellowship brain,
Small print obscure and sharp eye catching.
Let them be stethoscope testing,
   finger tip deceiving,
   and tendon hammer confusing

But solvable by secret skill:
  By special knowledge
    of the stop press news,
  by hunch or
    maybe microscope,
  by enzyme test, or
    fancy isotope,
  by 9 to 6 endeavour,
    late-night reading,
    postgraduate courses
    by the score.
  By the skin of his wife's teeth
    or tolerance,
  by the cliff edge
    of his overdraft.

And the Consultant?
Let it be something he has seen a hundred times
And others not at all:
  Something a gentle
    but strategic squeeze
  Pops back,
    a sophisticated sniff
  Unmasks,
    a tender touch
  Reveals,
    an apparently irrelevant question
  Unravels,
    such as "Did your mother
    ever eat caviar?"
  Eyes boggle, ears prick,
    elbows nudge,
  "Remember that."
  Trust Old Nosey to Know;
  He's done it again.

Wonder thickens
  and the merit award
  draws near.

¶ *W.C. Watson*

CARDIAC ARREST

Isoelectric silence,
suddenly stopped.
Starts the automated scramble
of intensive care –
Nurses pump
and frightened students
ready the apparatus.

Listen,
Upstairs and down
through endless corridors
races the dreaded code
of hope and terror.
It pushes into elevators
slides across the cafeteria floor
invades both sets of washrooms,
beats at the chapel door.
And like a costumed reveler
struck by the sudden panic
of his own disguise,
whips all it meets
into an anguished frenzy.

240 seconds.
Four fading minutes
to pay the awful debt,
the only one that ever matters
to a bankrupt brain.

Who knows
whether or not
within what's left
of those pathetic seconds
the clammy form
that was a man
will be made man again;

Who knows
whether it should?

¶ *Heinz Lehmann*

CODE

Three a.m. wake-up call,
Every intern's worst nightmare:
"Code 99 – ICU".
I sit up with a curse.
Two hours sleep, in installments,
Have ruined my temper.
Head thick with fatigue, I go hunting for shoes.
The gremlins have moved them.
I find one by the bedside . . .
Damn it all, where's the other?
Can't see in the dark . . .
Stumble into the hallway
Wondering God, who's the patient?
Hope it's not Mrs Murphy,
She was stable last night . . . .

ICU's in an uproar.
Must be thirty-five people
Not to mention the hardware drawn up by the bed.
In the midst of the chaos, the patient is hidden,
But I know the location.
Mrs Murphy. Of course.

Mrs Murphy is fifty-nine, fat, hypertensive.
It's her fourth major infarct
Her second arrest.
I'm to do CPR, so the resident tells me.
It's good practice for interns.
Keeps them out of his way.

So I rock back and forth with my hands on her sternum
While the technician bags and the monitor beeps
Counting seconds and praying
Please, God, let us save her,
I'm not that religious
Except times like these . . . .

We work for an hour.
The orderlies spell me.
Adrenalin, bicarb, a xylocaine drip,
Intubate, use the paddles
And none of it helping

Then . . . miracle! I see two wide-open eyes!

She can't speak, for the tube,
But I know that she sees me.
Her intern, her doctor, her angel in white.
She hungers to live,
But her weak heart has failed her.
We can't get it started.
It won't beat on its own.

No one else sees her face.
They don't know that she's conscious.
It's just her and me. God, her life's in my hands!
Then the resident mutters "Too bad, it's all over.
End of code. Call the family, I'll give them the news."

And I
Stop . . .

And watch while the light slowly fades in her eyes.
The others depart, but I stay by her bedside.
This code isn't finished. It's not time to go.

Leaden minutes creep by. There's no sound in the Unit.
I wait with my patient – for what, I don't know.
Then it comes: the sweet joy, the release, the forgiveness,
As her spirit flies free . . .
And at last, I'm alone.

¶ *M.E. Bramstrup*

CODE 444

As I walked down those midnight halls
All the lights were out.
Everybody had their pill
And no one was about.
Then from the walls a cry was heard
It pierced me like a chill:
Code 444, One East South,
It echoed loud and shrill.

Refrain:

Code 444,
Tell us which floor
So we can run and save
From a premature grave
Some poor soul standing at the heavenly door.

We came in minutes to the room
And found him on his back.
He was only 88,
A documented cardiac.
He had a tumour of the bowel
And what was even sadder
A teratoma of the lung,
Stones in his gall bladder,
Pyoderma of the skin,
An abscess in the brain,
A white-cell count of 22
– And Hodgkins was his name!

Refrain . . .

A tube was in the epiglottis,
His breath came from the Byrd,
Defibrillation didn't help
But we were not deterred!
Adrenaline, Bicarbonate,
He still could not be pegged;
Fluids through the cut-down
In his wooden leg . . .

Refrain . . .

¶ *Gerd Schneider*

HOUSE CALL: 3 A.M.

It's the daughter who telephones in the small hours,
waking the doctor because mother can't sleep,
the voice on the phone apologetic, yet demanding,
can "someone" bring pills,
bring sleep on the palm of my hand,
peace for the widow whose husband died today?
Oh, how I hated pill calls when I was an intern,
rolling out of bed with a curse,
why didn't the day doctor take care of it?
Now I've got to get dressed, get the car out,
the underground garage dark and dangerous at this hour,
they live at 70th and I live at 6th,
64 blocks with the street lights glaring down
on block after empty block;
I start to speed, anxious to get there and back,
zoom through the red light at 33rd,
really flying by 49th, don't even slow down this time,
the fifties going by in a blur,
then the sixties clock in, 64th, 65th,
got to ease up a bit now,
here's 70th, take the corner pretty fast,
then the apartment,
lit up for once and one of the daughters at the door,
the carpeted hall, here's the suite,
and here's the patient at the kitchen table,
drooping over her coffee, blowsy and red eyed,
she can't believe her careful bleach job
is all for nothing now,
she'll sleep alone from now on;
I give her the pills and a stiff "sorry"
knowing I should touch her shoulder but I don't want to;
my heart's not in it.
I leave and speed home through all the red lights
and am back in bed within twenty minutes,
thinking, Christ, I'm as bad as an intern.

¶   *Kirsten Emmott*

NIGHT SHIFTS

Blue black night sky shines
darker than a bruise.
Aurora borealis wheel
languorously overhead.

Persons seeking solace
or other cosmic rays of hope
walk or wheel in
to an all-night oasis
of healing and light.

Bright white countertops
and mudstained floors
without the warm smells
of coffee and donut grease.

The automatic doors open
to these celestial night bodies
who transubtantiate into patients
before ever changing their clothes.
They radiate earthly affliction.

Drunken man (bread knife in hand)
mistook his thumb
for a small salami.
"Sew me up."

Young woman complains bitterly
of pelvic pain:
always at 3 a.m.,
Only when the moon wanes.
She wants a needle
where it hurts the most.
"Please."

Fat man forgets
how to chew and swallow.
Is it possible?
He coughs and salivates
a tense story
of steak
chuck steak
chuck steak stuck
chunk of chuck steak stuck
big chunk of chuck steak stuck
in his gullet.
"Take it out."

Cabbie, itchy and scratching,
grows impatient
waiting for the last long run.
He recalls that cream
and the magic it worked
on his crabs
the time before.

"Got, ah, any of that crab cream?"

We are the late night
radio receivers.
In empty spaces
between the airwaves
other tormented souls
load guns,
plug in heating pads,
set clock radio alarms,
wait for sleep
and then walk in it,
clutch their hearts,
rock gently with the pain.

At the extreme reaches of the light
just beyond the turn of the radio dial,
a small search plane lifts off
for diseased parts unknown.

¶ *Vincent Hanlon*

SPINAL TAP

I toss and turn,
  It's uneasy sleep
A slow sinking into dreams,
  Then fitful awakenings.

Images of a child on the ward
  Keep breaking on my mind
"Febrile but not septic" – I am sure,
  Or am I?

My dreams are overcome
  With bacteria teeming in his blood,
Thick pus clouding his young brain
  Like a living net,
Oh Hell! The night is shot!
  I can't rest until I know.

Wearily pulling on clothes
  To face the cold night air
In the car, the long black road
  To the hospital --

The child is readied by the nurse.
  Bending over his arched back
I feel for hollows in his spine
  And sink the needle deftly:

Fluid runs out bright and clear
  As spring water,
Drips into cool thin plastic tubes.
He's bundled up and whisked away
Till the Lab tech phones:
  "No cells, no bugs."

So I head downstairs
  And out the door
To seize what's left
  Of the diminishing night.

¶ *Gerry Greenstone*

PRIMARY IATROGENIC PORTMANTOLOGIC DYSNOMENCLASIA

No Roman or Greek
Was ever heard to speak
Of adiadochokinesia; and so:
Our medical societies
Spent hours, out of piety,
Devising neo-classical lingo.
Now there's no need to hammer
Every fine point of grammar,
Nor to quote verbatim from Fowler;
Or debate like cognoscenti
Ad infinitum (or infiniti?)
Over 'datas' versus 'datum' or 'data'.
With congeni(men)tal block
Whether ergo propter hoc
Follows a posteriori – or not?

Thus, de facto usage
Is replete with abusage,
A more Iatrish than English novoglot.
So when your diagnosis
is "metabolic neutrosis"
(with no mention of a translator fee),
or when a phrase like "nephrotic
nephrosis'
leads to aural stenosis,
Then consider
Your poor patient's plea:

"Please say *what you mean*"
(Like in Alice's dream),
Stay away from the over-complex.
Please spare me the confusion
Of these classical allusions;
Veritas absolutus sermo
Ac semper et simplex."

¶ *Ian Wilkinson*

THE NAMING OF CELLS

(After the Manner of the Old Possum)†

The naming of cells is a difficult matter
Requiring complex cytological stains.
You may think that I am as mad as a hatter
When I tell you a cell must have three different names.
The first is the name that is descanted daily
Such as red cell or white cell, giant cell or round.
Such as large cell or small cell, benign or malignant,
Names that convey a quotidian sound.
But I tell you a cell needs a name in particular,
One more scientific and more dignified
Or else how can pathologists sound so oracular,
Apply for research funds or cherish their pride?
Of some of these names I can give you a quorum
Such as lymphocyte, macrophage (Langerhans' type),
Such as B-cell or T-cell or lymphoreticular,
Names that seldom belong to more than one cyte.
But above and beyond there's still one name left over
And that is the name which one rarely may guess
And genetic biologists strive to discover
What the cell itself knows and will never confess.
When you see a cell in a blast transformation
The reason I tell you is always the same.
It is deeply engaged in a rapt contemplation
Of the thought of the thought of the thought of its name.
It's molecular, nuclear, endonucleolar,
Deep and genetical NUCLEIC name!

†T.S. Eliot, "Old Possum's Book of Practical Cats"

¶ *James Gough*

METHUZELAM, CONFUZELAM

(Song of the detail man)

I find it so nostalgic when the Drug Man comes along;
His lecture takes me backward, like a dear old college song:
All hail, Alprazolam!
Bromazepam, Clonazepam,
Diazepam, Flurazepam –
Chlordiazepoxide!

I find them all so helpful when I go to my repose.
I utter them, and mutter them, until my eyelids close.

Should, shout: Lorazepam!
Oxazepam, Nitrazepam,
Temazepam, Triazolam,
And Carbamazepine!

In dreams the Drug Man will appear:
Sometimes in academic gown,
Or in the motley of a clown,
But always with his charming lear.
He says: "I have The Sponsor here
And he can make you very rich;
In fact, he'll give you half the take
From Lac Laronge to Kirkland Lake
(Sometimes the site is Lac LeBiche)

If you can answer: Which is which?

I sigh: "Who really gives a damn?
Alprazolam, Triazolam –
An azepine's an azepine."

Then I awake, still poor and lean.

¶ *Peter Grant*

INVASION OF THE MEGAMICE

You've seen it once, or maybe thrice:
Professor, labouring at night,
Over a gene he has to splice;

A shiv'ring scream!
A growling roar!
The Megamice break down the door.

The people flee.
The land is waste.
The military meet in haste
And grimly learn that no device
Is lethal to the Megamice.

A young researcher tells us that
He can create – the Megacat.

Such is the setting; such the Plot.
Now, the obligatory thought:
This is the twister, this is the sting:
Those Megacats eat everything . . .

¶ *Peter Grant*

CORPUS CALLOSUM

Nervous bridge
that binds these scraps,
copulator, integrator,
director of cathected buzz
or membranous cation flood,
tongue between worlds,
I aspire to you.

Specialists, risking vision:
dream calculators, lucid artists,
fallen priests, true saints,
know your slippery intersection.

A Buddha, corpulent and clever,
lounges on your chaise
unasking questions as they pass,
giggling at his interception.

Shared phallus,
the disparate are bound
in your flesh,
instantaneous as sex,
Nirvana – breathless,
you wait, old facilitator,
Janus, destroyer and creator,
Kiss me wordless now.

¶ *Bob Maunder*

KLEINSTEIN'S PHARMACY
PRESCRIPTIONS FILLED   COSMETICS   SUNDRIES

At closing, Kleinstein in his smock
surveys the papers of his trade,
assesses, reassesses, takes stock;
his time is spent
on coloured pills, well counted,
jokes repeated, people counselled
on the mixing up of pharmaceuticals,
things unsaid, decisions made.

What binds the bits of miscellany
in this store? Just Kleinstein
and his history hold the sundry
particles, chaotic malcontent
packages that claim safe sex,
relief from listed lesser pains,
shrinkage of warts and hemorrhoids,
clean drains, reversals
of the gracelessness of time.

Locked tight against the changing
nature of the neighbourhood and sidewalk swept,
Kleinstein's is finished for the night. Again,
along the same seven blocks
that have always led home, he walks
from Grandad's store to his house,
half-tenanted these days, a choice
he made when Gracie died.

Three generations' bric-a-brac
jumbled into his little space:
three months of *TIME* unread, a deck
of cards, TV guides, letters
unreplied, some saved to be reread,
strewn in concentric circles from his chair,
the only viewpoint from which
this chaos seems to fall in place.

At six a.m. Kleinstein returns,
puts on his smock and reassesses
inventory, reads the labels on the shelves,
looks out the window while his coffee
cools; plays out
this ritual; checks the newspaper
for headlines and obits.
Kleinstein prepares for business.

¶ *Bob Maunder*

AT THE SPECIALIST'S

"It was Dr. Lim who saw me,"
He told the receptionist.

*Have you been seen
by any other doctors*, she asked.

"I was elusive in those days,
staying far from the haunts of man,
but Dr. Lim glimpsed me
on the deserted road;
there'd been rumours,
he drove by at midnight,
his headlights caught
my pale face briefly
as he sped by.

"I followed him in the park;
he stopped to picnic
in a sunny field –
spread out his blanket
on a lawn of buttercups,
when he glanced up
to the edge of the woods
I dodged behind a tree.

"Dr. Lim in his backyard
underneath the summer stars
aimed his telescope
at the southern constellations;
there I was,
dancing on the moon.

"I took work as an extra,
I stood in crowd scenes,
the camera memorized me;
in the darkened theatre
my face grinned down
at the rows of faces,
Dr. Lim's among them.

"At last
I called on Dr. Lim.
he faced me,
he touched me
only with his stethoscope,
he stared over my shoulder
while my heartbeat had its say;
my legs swung nonchalantly.
He drew back.
He said:
'I'd like you
to see a specialist.
I'll ask Dr. Chan
to take a look at you.' "

¶ *Kirsten Emmott*

A POEM ABOUT THE PANCREAS

Even if you opened up a practice on Harley Street
no patient would come in with complaints
about his pancreas:
"I think it's my pancreas, Doc!"
– unless he too is a fellow professional
also educated
out of his natural mind;
few patients will be alarmed by the word,
not like "the heart"
words that summon up the feeling "le biscuit"
in the best of us.

Years from now
when you trundle in
thin and yellow, depressed
for abdominal films,
you too will have forgotten
your pancreas; and the news "It's cancer
of the pancreas" will hit
like an old family secret you knew all along;
"I'm sorry, but it's cancer
of the sweetbread"
'Not the Sweetbread!' – "Yes,
and, with proper medical management
early surgery
and a very rigid diet
you can look forward to at least
three months;" when the pancreas goes
it goes.

Those among us who are diabetic
whom the pancreas
torments by degrees
cannot help us conceive
of that familiar; even a poet
is at a loss for metaphor;
nothing short of a surgical exploration
will unearth
the thick spongey worm
twisted twice on itself
buried deep in the viscera
silent behind a curtain of peritoneum
– with a head, a body
and a tail,
using the man's face.

¶ *Ron Charach*

DUMMYTOLOGY

"Skin, It holds your insides in . . ."

Remembrances of Dr. H—, Clinical Professor
  and Head of "Dummytology,"
  a slight man with slick-backed hair
  like a gangster's from a grade-B movie,
  rhyming off his all-purpose maxims:
"If it's wet . . . Dry it,
  If it's dry . . . Wet it." Or,
  (meant to reassure our trembling patient
  but spoken with a knowing wink
  only an intern could notice):
"Not catchy . . . Not cancer."

Technicolour images
  from *The Atlas of God-Awful Things that Can Happen to Skin,*
  a compendium of acts of God, environmental hazard
  and bad genes: men with scales like fish,
  diaper rash so nasty you'd have to call in
  the Abuse Team, V.D. so advanced, so rotted away
  they must've had to cruise the Bowery
  to find it.
Skin like liver, skin like pizza,
  skin like chicken-liver pizza,
  combinations so crusty
  that even God would hold his cloudy stomach
  and wave away a few of those glossies.

Yet always the lure of Big Bucks,
   hardly any emergency call,
   a profession that still depends on the senses,
   and the hocus-pocus simplicity
   of steroid creams.
Or Agent Orange, Dry-'em-all-and-
   Let-God-Sort-'em-out approaches,
   like Accutane.

Biding time in the consulting room
   for that ever-elusive Big Catch:
   the little patch of suffered skin,
   shyly surrendered skin,
   that tells the expert eye a tale
   of unreported travels to faraway lands,
   that unravels the deadly mystery
   of injuries deep,
   and undercover.

¶ *Ron Charach*

ABRADED BACK

(On the Burn Unit)

In the Tank Room we are abraded back
past the point of thanks;
thought through the good skin left.
Skins that no longer cover our intent
buckle and fall to the floor,
shavings in a workshop.
This is a room for getting scrubbed dead.
Some point and mouth the O sign,
astonished by skull poking through
where face should be; some philosophize:
we are the ones in life who got burned.
No poetic wax; because the nurses work
long but depressed hours;
the men who clean the vats in masks may wink
and mean it,
but two have made the vegetarian switch
and no one smokes in bed.
At night an inner orderly wheels the psyche back
to the Tank Room,
room of the proud flesh, of the hero
watching cracks open up in his eschar
and not-crying, not-moaning, not-fainting;
In the Tank Room who gets scraped back
just to the point of thanks?

¶ *Ron Charach*

THE SCRUB NURSE

(An Anaesthetist's Dream)

Your cap conceals your hair
  from vulgar sight,
Just one dark curl
  all unrestrained lies,
Your mask hides nose and mouth,
  but gleams with light
The soft and slumbrous velvet
  of your eyes.

A little peek of smooth suntan
  is shown,
To prove that in the sun
  you've often laid,
I feel that buried just beneath
  that gown
Must surely lie the total
  nutbrown maid.

Would your mind blend in with mine
  like eggs with bacon?
Would your body tingle
  to a loving touch?
Would our hearts combine
  like dice that have been shaken?
Would you laugh at all my jokes
  but not too much?

But things are not as simple
  as they seem.
The ways of love are often filled
  with strife.
Before I turn to fact
  a lovely dream,
Perhaps I'd better go
  and ask my wife . . .

¶ *Barry Wheeler*

WHEN PERFORMING THIS TRICK IT'S ESSENTIAL
TO KEEP TALKING TO THE AUDIENCE

My body which once lightly
carried me has grown heavy lately
now I carry ungainly
its liquid machinery

and

even as I speak these words, two hazelnut
Florentines, three slices of Hungarian
salami and two hundred
cc of dry white wine
are holding communion in the acidic
darkness of my stomach

and

I remember a pair of dancers who wore
black kneepants and shirt and clown white
so that their limbs seemed as isolate
from their heads as Tuesday is from Thursday

or

as the corpse of an octagenarian on a slab
in the morgue is from the pleasure he had
when he recalled a particularly skillful play
he made once on a soccer field in his youth.

¶ *Arthur Clark*

131

was what he was.
She loved him (so she thought)
and when he died
she put on paper gown and rubber gloves
to find the thing that eluded her in life.
That first sliver slipped, Y-shaped
    zip
incision through his chest
and down his belly opened up
the heavy red drummy bump
off comes the breast plate
out come the heart
and lungs, in her hands she held
the remembered beating thing
dummy. Nope, not there, and
schlop schlop slurrp, up
comes the liver like a tub
of rubber silly putty nope
not that either, nor the long slippery
eel of glistening gut, which kept
trying to glide away from her rubber
fingers down the drain, drawn by the gurgle
in the pipes. "Oh, it's lovely and wet and –"
(wiping a tear with the sleeve of her gown)
"– but it's not what I thought I loved."

When the kidneys got sliced,
and the testicles too,
she went for the brain (having cracked
the skull-pot like a nut)
which she found abandoned
like some lost-on-the-coast-of-Acadian cabin
and she cried
    (as she snapped off her gloves)
    (as they folded the skin flaps over the cave of his chest)
    (as she ripped off her gown)
    (as they hosed his sweet red corpuscles down twinkling
        drainpipes)
"God! I just can't do this stuff any more!"

¶ *Arthur Clark*

132

SEX THERAPIST PRACTITIONER

Positions wanted.

We are looking
for bright young
self-motivating types
with demonstrated ability
to control ejaculation.
Past experience with
"Sensate Focus Four"
desirable but not essential.

Willingness to learn:
stop 'n start,
come 'n glow,
to squeeze or not to squeeze
the Sunkist orange;
anti-gravity manoeuvres,
moonlander,
genital touchdown;
contact sports,
by the light of the slithery moon,
see Spot, see Spot's dick's spots.

Fee for service
or contractual arrangement.
Binding arbitration.
Possible litigation.
Part-time.
Over-time.
Shift differential.

Reply with confidence
stating expectations.

¶ *Vincent Hanlon*

THE SURGEON

He comes striding through the ward,
Tries to look as if he's bored,
Students scatter as if frightened by a gun.
He inspects, then he palpates,
But he never auscultates
By a *proper* surgeon such a thing's not done!

Then he says, "My dear the knife
Is what you need to save your life,"
And he drapes her just as neatly as can be.
For five minutes of his leisure
He digs out her buried treasure
Then he mails her a substantial added fee.

¶ *Paul Steinhauer*

ON TAKING A HISTORY FROM AN ATTRACTIVE YOUNG WOMAN WITH A PORT-WINE STAIN ON THE LEFT BUTTOCK

Good morning dear,
I hear you have a mark upon your rear.
And you must tell me
Is it aching? Does it throb?
Does it hurt while on the job?
Does your type of occupation
Give you claim to compensation?
Does it bore?
Is it crampy? Is it burning? Is it sore?
Does it blanche when it is pressed?
Does it heal a bit with rest?
When you listen do you hear a strange bruit?
Or is that growl sound
Just a bowel sound,
Ma cherie?

¶ *Paul Steinhauer*

FACTORING THE CONVENTION

In 1 huge auditorium & $^1/_2$ of the Hilton's rooms:

Doctors who have the look of insurance-men

but a few of them distinguished, who parade

like high-class politicians;

me, throwing back the extra scotch, trying to be calm;

you and me, arguing about intercourse in our room.

1. (Look): (politicians) (like) (you and me)
   (arguing about intercourse).

2. (A few distinguished doctors) (trying) (intercourse)
   (in) (the) (huge auditorium).

3. (the extra scotch) (throwing back) (you and me)
   (and a few distinguished doctors) (to) (the) (insurance-men)

4. ($^1/_2$ the Hilton's rooms) (trying to be) (1 huge auditorium)
   (of) (Doctors) (trying to be high-class Doctors) (in) (the)
   (huge) (parade). (but) (you and me) (in our) (back) (room)
   (trying) (to be) (1).

5. (back) (to) (our room) (to) (have) (one) (extra) (look) (:)
   (have) (to be calm) (;)
   (–) (me) (trying) (and) (trying) (to) (be) ($^1/_2$) (of) (1).

¶ *Ron Charach*

CUTTING UP ONE NEUROSURGEON

My contempt
perseverates; I quote you as you are,
still centered in the needle-eye
   of auditory memory:
"Would you let this man . . . (our patient on his bed)
   . . . be an accountant?"
Then, grinning at your interns
   who were too ashamed to answer,
"I wouldn't let this man rake my leaves."

Kept your caseload as clean
   as your country-club.

Deep centers in the brain keep flashing you
Poised with your little black bag
   above a five-year-old with a tumour
   and down-turned eyes
   as his frozen parents heard you grumble
"Why do they waste my time with this case!"

You are not yet dead;
many are. *Do not breathe easy in your darkroom*
   smug about the speeded-up films of your heroics,
   the berries you plucked
   from favorable brains
Already they have retired your assistant TOO LATE

But they keep no real file
   on your invasiveness
   your metastatic entry into lives,
   the way you kept them hanging
   in the blue-tiled room

The sight of my longer hair made you turn away
   at a hall's length,
   so your shadow never fell on me; now,
   from the strength of these lucky years,
   – one final operation:
   To achieve what *you* always raved about:

That hard-to-get
   Deeper Exposure

¶ *Ron Charach*

137

PHILANTHROPY

Once the moment of dying
was caught by a physician
at the silent end of a tube.
The chest lay still,
the sated heart fulfilled,
blood stopped its flow
and the mottled skin
dispatched
a haunting memory,
gentle tracings of a life
gone still.

Now we summon the milling boys
with their reservoir
of bodies
for their separate parts.

The fate of their host
is in a world of many tests,
and the hope for the living
lies just beneath the shadow
of fresh death.

Dying beyond their means, and ours
shall be their living,
their very souls
lost in the swathing
of the new zeal.

¶ *Basil J. Grogono*

AN APPROACH TO DECLARING THE DEAD

As a medical student
I was in awe of the young interns
hastily called to the bedside of the recently dead.
It was their duty to assess the situation
and then declare, in writing, their conclusion.
The conclusion is always the same,
but the means to the end
is a matter of style.

Stethoscope to the silent chest,
forefinger on the impalpable pulse,
how shall it be done?
No one holds a chilled mirror
in front of the nose and mouth anymore.
I've tried these various methods
and found them wanting.
The problem is the medical curriculum
so tightly packed,
simply no time
for formal instruction in this area.
It must be an acquired skill.
I would argue however,
that it needn't be a 'hands on' experience.

Now, when I am called by a nurse
in the early morning hours
to declare a dead "patient" dead,
I take two steps into the "patient's" room;
I look at the face of death;
and then I know, deep in my non-medical bowels,
that here is a dead man.

"This man is dead," I say to myself.
I return to the nursing station
prepared to expedite the disposal of the remains
of another former member of the human race.
"Dead at 0615 hours," I write
on the doctor's orders sheet,
in the progress notes,
and on the certificate of death.
I sign my name legibly.

Of course, I can't recommend this approach
to the declaration of death for everyone,
but it works for me.

¶ *Vincent Hanlon*

140

REAL NUMBERS

After her 25th birthday
during the time of simple arithmetic
[before the new math]
my mother taught me
the value of real numbers.

I first counted the fullness of life as degrees of fever
    but I mistook its intensity
    for the insistent echo of a beating heart.
Later I learned to recognize life's swirling sweet symmetry
    in a hundred cooling butterhorns.
From her I discovered the exact proportions
    of water, sun, and fish fertilizer
    to extend the bloom of the rose.
Eventually she challenged me to calculate
    the length and breadth and depth of a marriage.

She taught me to tell time:
    when the curfew is broken,
    when to punch down the dough,
    when the membranes rupture,
    when they prayer goes unanswered,
    when the crocheted snowflake will melt.

Together now we confront more complex numbers:
    the annual statistics of the Canadian Cancer Society.

Patient and doctor we bravely,
mother and child we fearfully,
avoid each other's eyes
as we puzzle over
    "estimated new cancer cases by site"
    "five year survival rates" and
    "age-adjusted cancer death rates."
We let "x" be the unknown factor.

The truth of these negative numbers is clear,
opaque, unyielding,
self-evident.

But we yearn for a better brain,
a more sophisticated computer,
to find the error in our calculation,
or just a sharper pencil –
to scratch the numbers into our flesh,
to sketch the beauty of infinity plus one.

¶ *Vincent Hanlon*

DEATH OF A COWBOY

Pot bellied, lying in the snow,
Purple in the face, gasping for a breath,
His vomit still unfrozen on the ground,
Face to face with Death.

A weeping woman, a row of men,
Awkward, silent, standing by.
"Fifty did you say? It's a stroke you know.
Bad one, doesn't stand a chance."

"We found him Doc, like this – and let him lie
Beside the cattle squeeze.
Thought it best to leave him so, since you were on your way;
If we moved him he might die.

Poor old Hank, to finish here like this,
Blue in the face and gulping for his air.
Get that mattress over and lift him gently boys,
Though I doubt he knows we care.

That silver buckle on his belt Doc,
He won at some State Fair.
That – and his saddle in the bunkhouse there,
That's all there is, and none that's like to care.

Rodeo bum you might say.
And yet, he had his day.
Dam' good rider Hank, when he was young –
Good chore boy these few years.

Saddle broncs and pick-up man,
That's Hank's one claim to fame.
And now it's done, and none'll shed no tears.
Few years from now we won't recall his name.

Let's lift him gently boys,
And get him in,
Or he'll freeze
Beside this goddam squeeze."

¶ *Morris Gibson*

AFTER THE CONCERT

About this time of year my friends die:
Last fall poor Otto alone,
an old turtle listening for his private music
no longer on earth as he heard it
through his middle-Europe filter;
Mahler, Wagner and Mozart lay the canopy
over his three continents.

Maish,
tied to his humble machinery,
gauzes and distended veins, and drain pipes.
Everything else was shaved to essence,
his wise capacity
a grey skin brittle as the ash from his constant cigarette,
to make less of things.

And (at my age there will have to be an "and"),
O Edna who loves the music
of temporary talents and muscles that hoist sounds
for the frail moment;
as though there will always be a party . . .
An invisible pulse of perfume
laces the late night radio news:

It is now after the concert.

¶ *Vivian Rakoff*

SPACE-TIME'S MAIN

(In Memoriam, November 5, 1965)

(Beyond twenty years
Past occasional tears)
Before my very eyes
My own son dies.
(And my mistake
That's hard to take)

Though one thinks
One has covered over the chinks,
What's left behind
To haunt the mind
Is the suspicion
That nuclear fission
Relativity
And other trivia
Are but the tip,
Irrelevant chips
Off the warp of time
In Einstein's prosey rhyme.

That time is fraught
With mad distortions
Of vile proportion,
That now and forever,
Nothing can still
His cry of pain
Across space-time's main;
That his last breath
And painful death
Continue
To infinity.

¶ *J.V. O'Brien*

WHILE I LAY READING MEDICINE

Toddling alongside and staring up at him,
he strode so strong, so striking,
his head always gleaming because his hair was gone,
even then, when my wrist and his finger
were the same size
and he would stroke my wrist with his finger
inside the sleeve of my embroidered baby's dress
preserved in photographs
and memories across half a century.
What struck me most about Father
was his impulsivity,
He would strike while the iron was hot
– and luckily for us –
or our family would have been extinguished
in Poland, in the War.
He spoke fast, moved fast, ate fast,
drove erratically,
pronounced on whatever came to mind
embarrassing my mother
who was stricken
by improprieties.
And he was a fast decider,
cancelling contracts at the stroke of a pen
or promising his heart. On family outings
he sauntered half a block ahead,
the rest of us out of breath, straining
to catch up.

The blood must have hurtled through those stormy vessels
at the stroke of whatever hour it was
in the blue master bedroom of the house where
a quarter of a century ago
I studied anatomical connections and vascular disease,
when the string of connections – snapped.
It was that fast.
The stream inside his head got caught up,
disconnected,
diverted, while I lay reading medicine,

and he and I struck out.

¶ *Mary Seeman*

WHAT STAYS DOWN

What can you eat
What stays down
when the body tries to heave up its soul
like a plug –
for now you refuse the meal;
maybe tomorrow you'll be able;
these are dark days.

In room 4
one man who said no to lunch:
The well-known internist
who diagnosed his own leukemia;
while using his blood as normal blood
to compare with the ones being treated.
He must have let out quite an 'Oh no!'
for the night-staff
used to teasing him
about his late hours.
Did he first blame the microscope,
then the technician
for mixing up the slides
Was this someone's idea of a joke
Then the five pounds of weight he lost
became five separate losses,
and he Knew.
When you're forty-two
and the father of three;
when the house is almost paid for
and your boy starts to show
a little interest in medicine,
then what stays down
while you digest That news?

¶ *Ron Charach*

what if
the seed
as seed
grows   alien
to the self
as self
commuting
transience
through repetitive   disjunction
into awareness
of non-
existence
yet non-
disjunction   kills
and the genes
laugh
over dishonest
tears
for what never
was
yet is
as we are   were   will be

¶ *J. Lalouette*

DEAD CERTAINTY

As a child I was asked what I wanted to be,
"A doctor," I said without thinking.
I could not perceive
the death beyond my childish horizon.
Now a man, my limits are shrinking
all around, as death closes in.
Through my stethoscope I hear death's rattle
my rubber hammer falls from my hands
in battle; at each skirmish I lose
death raises a cheer;
though I cannot but leer
at his magnificent finality.
"You are a bad loser," he says, adding
"Why take sides against
dead certainty."

AN APPARITION

An apparition of you
I saw last night
as I listened to old Mrs F.
She wearily panting and sighing,
face paled by pneumonia,
small droopy breasts
cherry red nipples,
that once fed babies,
An apparition of you in years to come.
Tenderly my soul caresses her struggling breast,
glides up her neck and pallid pinched nose;
Till I know I will always love you.

¶ *Roy M. Salole*

149

THE DEAD

are busy holding up
the clouds in the blue sky
and putting little hydrogens
on carbons
and directing the traffic
from the violin string
to the tympanum and the heart,
pulling white light apart
and dealing out wavelengths
onto the evening gowns
modulating the glitter
the dead rustle cattle
and leaves and petticoats
and percolate through the whole
organic map:
"Keep it moving!"
they sing as they sock
another phosphate
into place and kick
an electron out of orbit.
They never rest
and here they'd thought
they'd have time to relax,
but no, they're busy as hell
and never have time to write.

¶ *Arthur Clark*

IN SEARCH OF MR GREEN

Everyone starts thinking
when they check on their basements'
slowly crumbling walls;
the plaster has been badly jobbed,
as if intentional.
As though it were the work of a single man
with a long-term plan.
And the sight of his platinum tie
rounding the corner in any dark room
at once informs
that the man can produce a razor in seconds.
The torsoes from a repeating dream
that plugged the holes in the walls of his ship
were cast by him;
and the way they were browned for firmness
was a sick-mind's work.
His back is bad from prowling after
straggling things, and his eyes
have a slow beat to the left
at rest.
His face is a hungry death-pie,
and the children know him better
than anyone.

Keep your eyes open
on the circular track;
Mr Green is out looking too.
Everyone has an estimate
of when he might suddenly gain.
One man whispers fondly to his arm
over the toothed machine,
another starts to slowly swerve
with a blow-torch in his hand.
Images of Mr Green
when the bone-capsule rubs on its own chips,
joint-life imitating crime.
Mr Green picks up interest,
says most deaths
make life look good
by comparison.

¶ *Ron Charach*

HOSPITAL ENCOUNTER

My heart is small
With valves that stem the tide
Of surges.
Like, not love, is what flows through.

That's true now
And was true then
Five years this spring

When I noticed you barely
In a roomful of people
A ripple in the river of routine.

I focus on that early meeting
Because it was fated
To open the flood-gates
Extraordinarily:

It was a hospital afternoon
In an academic conference;
My Sedentary habits
Had long ago occluded
Channels, possibilities,
When

A deluge,
Torrents of tremolo,
Inundations of magic

Waves of eros
With undertows of shame

All unexpected,
From an accidental meeting,
A sunset beam
Glossing off my hardening lenses,
To luminesce your youth;

For a time.
Till the irrigation grew artificial
And the swollen tributaries narrowed
to a trickle.
I settled for collegiality.

Now when I see you
In the hall
We talk shop,
And my pulse beats slow.

¶ *Mary Seeman*

A THERAPIST AND A ROSE

She carried it with care,
that blushing rose,
to my brown wooden desk.

Feeling the shy sweetness of its bloom,
learning of wounds deep in the heart,
we talked – as was our way each week,
of her sorrows and rage,
not knowing of my own.

I walked – as was my way each morning
to my brown wooden desk,
and met my blushing rose.
And then, as if to offer comfort
reached out my hand.

We exploded, my rose and I,
its petals scattering over the grainy wood
my tears, a shower trying to melt a heavy soul.
I wept: for her, for me, for love as lost
as a fallen rose.

¶ *Dorothy Hartsell*

FIRST VISIT

It hurts bad right here when I breathe,
I'm tired because I never sleep.
My knees make rusty noises when
I walk . . . the children never phone.
This little lump I never saw before –
You think it could be something bad?
Maybe it's better not to know . . .
My dog just died, so I'm alone . . .
Sometimes at night my heart beats fast
Like it could jump out from my chest,
And everything I eat or drink
Just sits there, heavy, like a stone.
Last week I coughed and there was blood;
I'd throw the cigarettes away
But it's too late to help me now . . .
So fast, like smoke the years have blown . . .

Too many losses, too few gains;
Too much gone wrong, too many pains . . .
Too much unasked, too much unsaid –
And worst of all – too much unknown . . . .

¶ *Maurice Schwartz*

STRICKEN BY FLU

Never again shall I think "Weakling"
of a 200 pound construction worker
who wanders in with runny nose and sore muscles
forehead bursting, drums popping,
eyes turbid as Murano glass.

In a way I am better off than him
with my own theoretical
if not immunologic defenses:
It's simply been (again) the wrong virus strain
for which I received vaccination
(I'll tell you later
if this affects my views
about vaccination on a larger scale).

But today I'll try anything,
folklore nostrums and pharmaca alike,
chicken soup, tea with honey,
and Extra Strength Tylenol (pray, without the cyanide)
but most of all I believe
in Triaminicin with Codeine
that my local pharmacy
is always running low on.

But in truth, I enjoy being pampered
in bed with the flu, exercising my right
of every human to be sick . . .

And tomorrow, when one of my patients,
trying to be funny, asks
"How come a doc gets sick?"
I'll throw him the age-old dictum
"Yeah, Sometimes doctors even die . . ."

Viruses creep into our lives, and go,
but first play on all of our frailties;
and it's not so bad
so long as they leave us healed,
and more sensitive to prostration
in all our fellow men.

¶ *Mladen Seidl*

156

I STEPPED PAST YOUR ROOM TODAY

I stepped past your room today
  Rushed to a crammed office
Rather than endure
  The eerie calm of Palliative Care
It's been three days now
  Since I visited you
And that's not good.

I was there from the beginning
  When we split your belly
To find cancer
  Erupting everywhere
The liver's glistening surface
  Ridged and spotted as the moon.

Then came the radiation
Malignant clusters beamed with cobalt
Bombarded with pions,
In a cellular explosion.
And chemotherapy
Specialized molecules
To invade you like tissue
And work their complex chemistry.

But in the end
Our white-coated arsenal
Was powerless
Against the long trajectory
Of disease.

Now you lie there
  Shriveled husk of a man
So pale and trembling
  With barely enough weight
To press against the sheets.

In the harsh glare of those white sheets
  I see the impotence
Of myself as a physician
  Whose energy is aimed
At cure and renewal.
  Can you understand
What it means to face you
  Like this,
Your courage against my fear?

Let me not lose sight
Of what you once were
And still are
A man and a father
Who did the things fathers do
Watched your daughter at ballet
Her leaps and pirouettes
Cheered your son at his soccer games
Stood shivering in the rain.

To respect your humanity
To preserve your dignity
Because if I can hold you clear enough
There's nothing more to fear.

¶ *Gerry Greenstone*

INFERNO

Tonight I'm face-to-face
with a man
who has just been burnt alive.
The destruction of his skin
is so complete
he is left painfree
and strangely composed.
He shivers with cold.

To a barrage of questions
he chooses to say very little.
I watch his eyes
fixed on my left hand
as it slides the intravenous needle
into him.

Ten minutes ago we were strangers.
Now, still strangers,
I use his first name
as if we knew each other.
"Give Stan 10 milligrams of morphine slowly, please."
Indignities great and small,
all one to him,
whose skin is thick
and grey
and senseless.

In his eyes
I see the flames die down
but I'm forced to turn my face
from the inferno's heat.

¶   *Vincent Hanlon*

THE STETHOSCOPE'S SONG

His patient's chest gave a few friendly heaves
With the sound coming through as a typical wheeze.
Then with delight he heard music and words
(Ignoring the fact that this was absurd).

He explained to his "shrink" it was all quite benign
And that in fact he was perfectly fine.
He worked every day and earned a good dollar
Looking perfectly normal in suit, tie and collar.

But the moment the last of his patients had gone
He'd fine tune his stethoscope to an up tempo song,
And night after night the singers would say
    "You performed like a genius again today!"

¶ *Carl Lapp*

THE NAKED PHYSICIAN

"Physician, Feel thyself"
laughs the bathroom mirror
as opaque as a blind, as he prepares
  to rush away again.
The dimmed track-lights barely surface
  the Man-sized Kleenex and the K-Y,
  a weightless space-age telephone
  that kept them all from sleeping well,
  and fitted sheets that will do their best
  to carry him out when it's *his* turn.
The floor carpeted in a silence
  that pulls at the walls, reminds him
  there are no more laurels to strain for.

In a small black bag
  the rubber tube with the metal arms relaxes,
  always willing to listen;
  the ancient rubber cuff is still a hand
    with a measured grasp;
  what others need, and all he really owns
    lies deep in the case of desertion.
Now and then the needle in the gauge
  eases up on its own, as if hungry
  for witnesses who will swear:
  "He had a manner, He held my wrist
    firmly but gently, He used to make house-calls"
or simply: "Into
  the cold white winter day
  went his fur-collared coat."

Only his final rut and rash manner
  with the only ones he ever failed,
  his family, will be recorded

in the final light.

Though a surviving son can take comfort:

"Your father was, by all reports,
a dedicated man."

¶ *Ron Charach*

161

FAULKNER FALTERING

Faulkner hauls his head off his arm,
his catnap leaves behind a blotch
a mark of Cain on a man
 who naps on lunchbreaks.
His face is itching to break out;
 by tomorrow he'll look eighteen again.
Strange, even after forty years of saving face
the blemishes persist   like gauges,
like an impasse.
And while his linen shirt is precious
 its collar hugs his throat
 like a heavily jewelled hand;
though it did look good in the shop window,
 five autumny colours blending, a loose enough fit
 to leave room for the inevitable –
No longer special, it's one more item
 to swell the laundry pick-up bag,
 one more Handle with Care for Lee Duck Chan.
And while his belly is squeezed to a camel's back
 by his belt, and is a trifle grotesque,
 last week's five pound weight loss
 would have once meant success.

Faulkner is late for his massage at The Club;
his one o'clock patient will have to come to grips
 with waiting. Faulkner's *thing*
 is making his patients wait,
 giving them one more task in maturity,
 and he denies that it's easier
 on *him* that way.
This afternoon would have him see two men
 who are full of themselves, and three women
 who are full of someone else. Just yesterday
 two grief reactions that differed only in the names;
 like a slew of pediatric red throats.

There's something sexless about grief.
And, goodness knows, even I,
who get to live with a little variety,
have to face my own pain alone.
And there's plenty of that. Because Faulkner's world
  has become a hard dry piece of cheese,
  and he's not in the mood
  for seconds.
  thought I'd eat a yard of her shit
  for ten minutes more of her time.
His lower back has been temperamental
  since she left him, Seven weeks ago today.
No point being gentle.
No sweet patience can dam the surge
  that sweeps his long face
  breaking across his forehead,
  settling out in motley red markings.
Anything in sight will do for a cross:
  the shirt, the office, his belly or his belt,
  even the blessed occupation – psycho-therapist,
what a joke
patient after patient after patient
  with unending complaints,
  when so much has to go into just trying
    to stay alive, on the job,
    and away from a gun.
Faulkner is an American.

Suppertime is a distraction.
Heating through a bowl of soup, he ends up
  calling for a pizza,
  to be delivered Soon, please,
  to DOCTOR Faulkner (maybe good
  for extra cheese) –
Picks up a red felt marker – *beats blood –*
  and turns her favorite tablecloth
  into a graphics display.

And though he frowns on irreversible gestures,
   he prints straight on the linen:
About how his love started changing,
about how jealously he watched Mark play guitar,
casing him for things that might interest her.
How he charted her comings and goings
   like a tornado's
Would you suddenly shift course
and attack me with the same force
we both used on your old lovers?
But he steps from the parentheses
   of the kitchen-game,
      decides to forego the drudgery of reviewing his notes
   on tomorrow's endless patient-load
For a glass of Southern on the rocks,
   tall as mercy.

Again it's time to make the room spin
   with Southern.
Becoming quite the drinker in my middle age.
Heads into the sunken living-room
   and greets the golden bottle in the hideaway bar:
You gave me more than I dreamed a drink could give.
   Knowing he's still talking to her,
      that for weeks all he sees and says is her,
regret spread through him
   like pungent wine.
If he'd have only opened up . . .
   like someone real –
In the fridge there's only hard dry cheese
   in a moody compartment;   ·
the table starts to pull at him
   like an iron thing.
To sign off, with something better
   than self-pity, which he's seen so often
   in patients.

But he has to print: *O LAURA!*
no less ridiculous than the horse and carriage
   on the bottle.
Go down to the sofa, push the button on the TV,
   and buy time.
Southern a fine anaesthetic for the heart,
   as the sleep of late-night TV is
   for the brain.

¶ *Ron Charach*

MY VISION

I live with the vision of my brothers and sisters
parents and grandparents
on the truck to the gas chambers
and see them
billowing in the sky.

I live with twice daily selections
of emaciated colleagues-musselmen
and their frantic attempt to
appear strong and healthy in spite of buttocks
devoid of gluteus maximus
amidst starvation, typhus and dysentry.

I live with the knowledge
that so long as they avoid selection
the possibility of life for one frightened, confused
but healthy soul,
disembarking
from the newly arrived train
is extinguished.

I live with the obsession
of ensuring that they not develop sores or ulcers
amid lice, scabies and beatings,
since such signs would mean
special treatment
with Zyklon B.

I live with their cooperation with science –
with artificial burns, effects of drinking sea water,
experiments in cold immersion in freezing water,
experiments with mustard gas,
artificially induced typhus, hepatitis and malaria;
experimental sterilization with removal of testes
and injection of caustic substances
without anesthesia
into cervix and uterus.
I cannot talk about these
things,
nor can I expect people to understand

How do I share such horror.
How do I make my children understand
why I am the way I am.

Why would I want them to know
what I know
see what they saw
relive what they relive nightly
Why should I awake the dead
within me;

I want them
to know me.

¶ *Daniel Lowe*

NAZI DOCTORS

Hippocrates
sat
frozen as he witnessed
the orgy of caring
for the health of the Volk
by disciples
in black hoods and lab coats;
their malignant service:
white coats
over SS boots
removing
white roses
forever.

¶ *Daniel Lowe*

A SITTING SISYPHUS

rowing
a mechanical boat
in the basement
on a sea
of tiled floor
the mind drifts
to unreachable ports

the body restrained
to the mere
to and fro
sweat forms
quicker these years
a heart thumps
and races
near the limits
of middle-age

and for a half-an-hour
at this time of day
at this time of life
finally it feels good
to be going
nowhere

¶ *Shel Krakofsky*

IN A BICYCLE REPAIR SHOP

bent and missing
spokes
among rusted and
inadequate frames
battered brakes
emaciated tires
piled up
and tangled
like the bodies
in mass graves
impossible to be
put together again
like the survivors
who line
their therapists'
bicycle shops
with the same chance
of being reassembled
and repaired

¶ *Shel Krakofsky*

CHURCH STREET BOOKSTORE, A TORONTO REUNION

"You're Velvel."
"I go by Vernon now. Didn't you
used to be Shmuel?"
"Still am."

He caught the smugness, a sensitive boy
who avoided the before and after
Hebrew school sports, a bookish pacifist
before the rest of us cared what
books and non-violence were all about.

Doing his job, Vernon found
the requested book
little talk from his pale, bony face
no sideburns sprouted from
the finely cut short hair
razor nicks along the straight back edge
where his hair stopped
to meet the flesh of skull.

A *cheder* dropout
he learned the essence
of the curriculum anyway
with a labelled can
beside the electronic
cash register.

After counting the change
I
drop
eighteen
cents
in
his
pushka
marked
AIDS.

To life. Maybe Velvel's.

¶ *Shel Krakofsky*

COUNTERTRANSFERENCE CALL

Ring! Ring! Ring!
"Hello," I answer politely.

"Yes, Is this the Doctor?" asks the nervous
  voice of an old lady.
"Yes, is there anything I can do?"

She pauses for a while,
  coughs gently, and having heard me right
  slowly puts the phone aside.

She does this almost every night
just when I'm half-asleep,
dogtired from Jeffreys Clinic.
At times I wait for her,
  half-aware of a torment I can no longer bear.

Ring! Ring! Ring!
"Hello", I say, pausing.

"Is this the Doctor?" She coughs a little
  but this does not matter anymore.
"Dammit!" I shout, "You old bogey!"

It must have shocked her,
  just as this unusual burst of temper
  chills my innermost nature.
The telephone keeps falling down
  and coming up, shaking and trembling on the rack.
At last, relief comes to me
  like a calm day after a storm.

But as night after night
  passes behind my windowsill,
time wears, and leaves me cold in the dark
  with a shaken will.

Surely, I tell myself,
something must have gone wrong
for any doctor to silence any call.

The old are not always sick;
  to hear a reassuring word
  is sometimes all they need
  to sleep well, and brave
  the night of old age.

Ring! Ring! Ring!
"Hello," I say kindly.

"Is this the Doctor?"
"Yes," I answer sweetly, "Is there
  anything I can help you with?"

She pauses for a while,
  coughs a little
  and knowing that she's heard me right
  she bangs down the phone with all her might,
  sending explosions
  through the shadowed lanes of my mind;
I cower and cringe in pain.

But after a while
  another relief comes on,
  like a grace after sin.

¶ *Elmer Abear*

FROM THE CLINIC WINDOW, POND INLET NWT

Bylot island is the rock-god's body,
barren paradise.
Rock heights that keep humans small
part, as God might part Her garments,
let the glaciers flow to ice sea,
pure cold milk of God
that flows, flows yet seems still
to eyes that cannot keep the time of rocks.

Reflected in the window, clinic life
counts time in human sounds, cries,
clatter of the implements of care,
the phone, the plane whose drone brings mail
and takes the Med-Evacs down south.

I close the door. Between these lives
another story clucks out in Inuktitut
words that stab and pluck at air,
this strange percussive instrument
for tales suspended in ancestral lives,
in one long winter night, alive with spirits,
whole and untimed.

My body, slumped in its chair,
becomes a passive thing, a bowl,
a soft receptacle for pain,
an ear, an echo-cave.
I hear, a story needs an ear,
the harp-song words, resonant until translated,
filled with meaning, heavy, silent
stories for my concavity.

¶ *Bob Maunder*

HEART SONG

Dance now, your heart beats jazz,
  life fibrillates, skips, pauses,
  lingers, lets the breath return,
  stops breath.
Drown dancing. Spin. The music eddies.
Soon the pool will warm,
  grow wormy, still,
  too slow for vertebrates,
  invertebrates will wind your bones.
Return to sleep, my friend.
Unsyncopated hours will crack you
  like a ribspreader; your dance,
  its tissue metronome exposed,
  intones "Don't stop, don't stop, don't stop, don't stop."

Wake. You know the beat by heart,
  the flagellate imagination.
Escape the anaesthetic breath
  to cold creative oxygen.
Explode.

Antichrist, you celebrate
  when dancers fall, when lakes
  are beaten celibate, warm, static,
  when whales can't copulate
  in waters warm and wormy.
Do not roll over used to dancing, friend.
  Unsyncopated hours will
  turn your heart to rubber,
  warm and calm your liquid madness
  sings "Don't stop, don't stop, don't stop."

¶ *Bob Maunder*

HYMN

All the little outlets of the house are singing
Gloria in Electricitas! a chorus
picked up in ecstasy by the pop-up toaster,
and the grill and the refrigerator join in singing
Gloria! The lights are plugged in, the blender
is filled with the spirit, the transformers are humming,
the power lines are filled with Gloria!
and all the appliances harmonize Glo-ri-a!
The radio is near the edge of the shelf above me
as I sit in the tub singing one of my favorite commercials
and in the apartment upstairs a beautiful young musician
is playing Liebestraum with feeling.
My corpuscles samba through my capillaries
and the musician's corpuscles samba through her capillaries
and my heart and her heart
achieve precisely the counterpoint
I wanted in this counterpoint:

  Hallelujah!
  Hallelujah!

You have to listen closely, long to hear.

¶ *Arthur Clark*

ORIGAMI

At first, a long tie ago,
there were only the folds of your armpits
and your buttocks and groin and eyes,
then the folds of the palms
whereby Madame Ricardo purported to know your future.
Much later came two folds on the forehead.
The folds at the eyes extended,
the ones between the nose and lip grew deep.
More folding. Vertical folds crossed the horizontal,
summers folded onto autumns, and the year
was folded by year and put on year away.
Vast sorrows were folded onto minor triumphs,
tucked under the slip of memory and lost.
Then I began to see the process,
in long shadows, by altered evening light,
as a process, and how each folding
brings you closer to perfection of the finished piece.

¶ *Arthur Clark*

"I fished around inside the bodies
of good dead men, and could find nothing
but my own fear, my own disappointment"

After midnight in the Gross anatomy lab,
cramming

God forbids the middle ear;
you are here to explore only the larger stations,
refusing to see them as they once saw themselves.
Women. Men. In formalin.
On cool metal tables, catch their deaths . . .
Tables so short you might never guess their purpose,
blindfolded. But then, many come from India.
Infant skeletons a major export.
Their organs pulled out for inspection
then put back in their cases. How many
might still play well inside other bodies?
Though after midnight these dead get up,
to play tennis,
the Prosects against the Dissects;
at first the Prosects always lose
– their cut muscles flapping from their bones,
but gradually . . . gradually . . .
the Dissects start losing a muscle here, a nerve there
pectoralis major, then *minor*,
so if you catch the game late enough in the term
it's a toss-up
who wins.

Scratching with his scissors for Fallopian tubes

Searching for life in the late hours,
the rest of the class gone home for the good sleep,
leaving behind their pure white suits
in a pile.
On the particular day they did *the face*
he came down with something,
and had to miss the lesson.
Something in his own body knew that the lipless grit
would forever make watering the specimens
more difficult. Like a game of mime,
warm water trickling through a punched-out spout;
pretends he's watering plants; his mind
dousing their heads with humour. Vegetables.

Each of twelve remember

throbbing in the now empty
thoracic cage. And if a cage,
for what variety of bird
that must sing sweetly in love
yet eat its way through meat
for the final escape.
And what degree of animal
must the skull contain.
Twelve well-preserved women and men going bad
their thin beams up in stirrups
a unisex clinic, full of tampon-remover jokes,
whores in the wrong hands . . .

By morning the skylight buys back the room

for the living.
I return to my favorite body, his face
behind the flat green drape.
While his mask was still attached
he wore a long thin reed of a moustache
waxed up at the ends
and was nicknamed the Colonel.
With not a single extra ounce of fat
– must have had cancer.
Yet he is the colonel still, *my* colonel
and acquiescing cadaver;
and when he willed his husk
to teach me, he too
had wanted to rise and meet
the basic science.
Through the silent shroud:
A tear for what we are, and must be,
might still be squeezing through
the tiny twisted canals
even while the two of us
explore –

¶ *Ron Charach*

ELMER ABEAR is a general practitioner who lives in Lourdes, Newfoundland.

ARIEL BOILEN lives and practises medicine in Madeira Park, British Columbia. She has contributed to "The Physician as Patient" column in *The Medical Post* and to a special supplement on women in medicine.

M.A. BRAMSTRUP is a family practitioner who lives in Fredericton, New Brunswick. She is an accomplished author with several science fiction novels and medical humour books in print as well as a comic book series.

RON CHARACH, born in Winnipeg, Manitoba, is a practising psychiatrist and poet who lives in Toronto. He is author of *The Big Life Painting* (Quarry Press) and editor of "The Medical Poet" column in *The Medical Post*.

ARTHUR CLARK is a neurologist who emigrated from the United States to practise in Calgary, Alberta. His first collection of poems, *Kinetic Mustache* (Véhicule Press), was published in 1989.

ROBBIE NEWTON DRUMMOND is a family doctor practising in the Crows Nest Pass region of Alberta. He was born in Montreal and studied medicine at McGill University. His poems have appeared in the anthologies *Poets 88* (Quarry Press) and *Sounds New* (Muses' Company) as well as in such literary magazines as *The Fiddlehead, Grain, Prism,* and *Arc.*

KIRSTEN EMMOTT was born in Edmonton, Alberta, and studied medicine at the University of British Columbia in Vancouver, where she now conducts her practice. She is a member of the Vancouver Industrial Writers' Union whose poetry has appeared in the anthologies *Going for Coffee, A Government Job at Last, New Voices,* and *Shop Talk.*

MORRIS GIBSON, born in Scotland and educated at Glasgow University, is an internationally renowned author of books about the lives of doctors who lives near Courtenay, British Columbia.

H.J. GOLDSTEIN was born in Toronto and studied medicine at the University of Ottawa, where he co-founded the medical show "Euphoria." He is a general practitioner at York-Finch General Hospital whose life-long ambition is to write.

JAMES GOUGH works as a pathologist at the University of Manitoba Health Science Centre in Winnipeg, Manitoba. Born in Ireland and graduated from Trinity College, Dublin, he has published articles in pathology journals as well as features on medicine and literature in *The Medical Post.*

PETER GRANT was born in India, matriculated from Upper Canada College, and graduated with a degree in medicine and psychiatry from the University of Toronto. He is the Director of Psychiatric In-Patient Services at St. Catharines General Hospital who has won limerick writing contests.

GERRY GREENSTONE was born in Dublin, Ireland, and moved to Canada in 1951. He studied medicine at McGill University and now practises as a pediatrician in British Columbia. His poems and articles have been published in *The Medical Post* as well as in the Newsletter of Canadian Physicians for the Prevention of Nuclear War.

BASIL J. GROGONO was born near Cambridge, England, and studied medicine at St. Mary's Medical School in London. He is an orthopedic surgeon who practices in Halifax, Nova Scotia, and in Bermuda. He is editor of *The Nova Scotia Medical Journal.*

VINCENT HANLON grew up in Calgary, where he completed a Master of Arts degree in English Literature at the University of Calgary before studying medicine. He works as an emergency physician in Fort McMurray, Alberta. Several of his poems have been presented in a work entitled "Only Blood Stains: The Making of a Doctor" at the Edmonton Fringe Festival.

DOROTHY HARTSELL was born in St.Thomas, Ontario, and graduated from the University of Western Ontario before studying medicine at the University of Toronto. She now practises psychiatry in Toronto.

SHEL KRAKOFSKY is a family doctor who lives on farm in Komoka, Ontario. His poetry has appeared in The League of Canadian Poets anthology *Garden Varieties,* and his fiction has been published in *The Toronto Star.*

CARL LAPP lives in London, Ontario, where he practises psychiatry.

J. LALOUETTE practises medicine in Sault Ste. Marie, Ontario. His poems have appeared in major Canadian literary magazines, including *Poetry Canada Review.* He has published a chapbook, *Agawa and Other Poems* (Penumbra Press), and a book, *Lights Over the River* (Mosaic Press).

HEINZ LEHMANN was born in Berlin, Germany, and studied at Freiburg, Marburg, Vienna, and Berlin Universities before emigrating to Canada. He is Professor Emeritus at McGill University and a recipient of the Order of Canada whose research in psychopharmacology is world renowned.

DANIEL LOWE practises dermatology in London and Toronto. He was born in Montreal and educated at Jewish Peretz School, Northmount High, and McGill University. His poetry and essays have appeared in *McGill Page, Avotaynu,* and *Viewpoints Literary Supplement.*

BOB MAUNDER is a psychiatrist and poet who lives in Toronto.

J.V. O'BRIEN was born in England and reared in Ireland where he attended Trinity College, Dublin. He practises as a psychiatrist in Nova Scotia and contributes occasional articles to *The Medical Post.*

VIVIAN RAKOFF was born in South Africa and educated in Cape Town, London, and Montreal. An accomplished author, he has written poems, essays, plays, and film documentaries apart from his professional psychiatric writing.

CARL J. ROTHSCHILD is a child and family psychiatrist who was born in Washington, D.C., and now lives in Vancouver, B.C. He is a Clinical Professor at the University of British Columbia whose poetry has been published in various small magazines.

182

ROY M. SALOLE, born in Aden, South Yemen, studied medicine in London, England. He practises psychiatry in Ottawa.

MAURICE SCHWARTZ is a family practitioner who lives in Montreal. A graduate of Strathcona Academy and Queen's University, he served with the Canadian Infantry in World War II before earning his doctorate from the Sorbonne in Paris.

MARY SEEMAN is Psychiatrist-in-Chief at Mt. Sinai Hospital in Toronto and Professor of Psychiatry at the University of Toronto. She was born in Poland and has written articles and books on psychiatry, with special focus on schizophrenia.

MLADEN SEIDL was born, raised, and educated in Zagreb, Croatia, Yugoslavia. He has been an active writer of poetry, fiction, and art reviews since his youth. He has a family practice in Toronto.

GERD SCHNEIDER is Editor of the Newsletter of the Canadian Physicians for the Prevention of Nuclear War who practises medicine in Ottawa. He was born in Germany and studied at the University of Toronto. His study of home births published in *Canadian Family Physician* received the Research Prize in 1987.

ROBERT W. SHEPHERD was born in Argentina and served as a pilot in the Royal Canadian Air Force. He practises psychiatry in the Eastern Townships of Quebec and writes for various magazines, including *Redbook* and *Vogue*. He is working on a book for women entitled "Reclaiming the Authentic Self."

PAUL STEINHAUER is a child and adolescent psychiatrist from Toronto widely known for his work in family therapy. He is also a pianist and song-writer whose poems included in this anthology were originally performed in a medical school satirical review.

BETTY UJANEN lives in Sault Ste. Marie, Ontario, where she practises family medicine.

W.C. WATSON, born and educated in Glasgow, Scotland, has practised medicine in the United Kingdom, Hong Kong, the United States, Kenya, and London, Ontario. His short stories have been published in *Canadian Doctor*. He is the discoverer of "Bingo Brain."

HEATHER WEIR, born in Dublin, Ireland, now practises psychiatry in Toronto, specializing in the treatment of adolescents.

BARRY WHEELER was born in England and educated at Epsom College, Surrey, and at St. Bartholomew's Hospital Medical School, London. He has worked for the medical branch of the Royal Air Force and now practises in Truro, Nova Scotia. His poetry has appeared in *The Pottersfield Portfolio*.

JOE WIATROWSKI is an emergency physician who lives in Winnipeg, Manitoba.

IAN WILKINSON was born in England and now works as a biochemist at Sunnybrook Hospital in Toronto. He writes for *The Medical Post, Urinalysis News*, and other publications.